THE BIPOLAR PRESIDENT

CHRIS MORKIDES

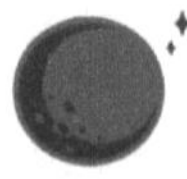

DEDICATION

For brave people battling mental illness daily

Others can see a broken leg. They can't see bipolar, but it hurts so much more.

CHAPTER 1

I owned that city.

From City Hall to Billy Penn and his hat sitting atop City Hall, to the Liberty Bell, which I couldn't see but thought I could hear gonging for me as I crossed the Walnut Street Bridge on my way to Rick's Center City apartment to tell him the good news.

I owned that fucking city. Hell, Billy should have given me his hat so I could spook the doorman before he sent me up to Rick's apartment to give him the good – no, monumental – news.

I won my first case that day. Five months out of law school, the junior member of a five-lawyer team, trying an Equal Pay Act case in federal court in Delaware. Maybe I should have spread the credit, but I was the one who won it, not the other four who plotted trial strategy – I was there, half-listening – before we went into court to take on the State of Delaware, which refused to pay nurses the same amount as a male physician's assistant who was doing the same work. The fact that we were in court in the first place was a mild upset. The judge tossed our case on summary judgment before I wrote a brilliant brief showing the judge the error of her ways.

The other lawyers on my team, one after another, questioned witnesses during the first few days of the trial exactly as we planned. It was all I could do to stay awake and, if I read the jury correctly, it was all they could do to stay awake, too.

But they were wide awake when I strode to the lectern because, well, my questioning didn't follow the script. You're not supposed to ask leading questions of your own witnesses, but that's all I did. After we discussed trial strategy the night before the trial, I went to my room, tried unsuccessfully to get to sleep and decided that I would bend courtroom rules and see if I could get away with asking leading questions while making the questions sound non-leading. I got away with it until the State's lawyers objected sometime around my fifth or sixth witness and the judge, correctly for once, sustained their objection.

But the cow – or horse; I always get this confused – already was out of the barn and we won the case. Hell, we – I mean, me – did more than win. I got double damages, which you only get if you prove that the other side really, really screwed up.

And that's what I told Rick when I finally reached his apartment. Before I got there, though, I stood halfway across the bridge, surveying Philadelphia, looking out at the Schuylkill River, winking at Billy Penn, listening to the Liberty Bell play my favorite song – "La-La Means I Love You," by the Delfonics – on the most magical night of my life.

I have bipolar disorder.

I truly believed I owned the city that night nearly 40 years ago.

I truly believed that I owned the city when I was elected mayor of Philadelphia after serving as District Attorney for 10 years.

I truly believed that I owned the state of Pennsylvania after I was elected governor.

And now that 1600 Pennsylvania Avenue, Washington, D.C. is my address – I would have preferred more informal digs, but they make all presidents stay here -- I sometimes believe that I own the country.

Not most of the time, though. I usually take my meds.

CHAPTER 2

Watch White House news the way I used to watch White House news and there is one thing that stands out in the Oval Office. The desk.

The President, which would be me for the moment, usually is sitting behind it, signing some sort of important bill, a lot of fawning congressmen and congresswomen around him and an American flag in the background.

The president looks important, which is the point. The congressmen and congresswomen look important, which is the point. And the desk looks important, which is the point.

I wish it wasn't the point, but it's true. I enlisted the help of a couple of big, burly Secret Service agents to move the desk on a day when I wasn't signing a bill, but it was too heavy. So, here it sits, not far from the Presidential Seal and Abe Lincoln's portrait. Abe sometimes sneaks on camera if you watch White House news the way I used to watch White House news before I started living here, but the cameras tend to focus on me.

My wife, Ariana, hates that desk, too, So, Ariana and I work around it during the most important part of my day: our morning talks. We've set up a couple of comfy chairs, one ottoman for me to rest my aching knees on, and a coffee table by the window overlooking the Rose Garden. You won't see our additions on the evening news because we wheel them away before the cameramen come in.

"You sleep alright last night?" Ariana asks me as we sip coffee and look out the window at the Rose Garden. They really do have a good landscaping service here, better than the one I had at the governor's mansion in Harrisburg.

"As good as I'll ever sleep until after the summit."

"You're not going down that rabbit hole again this morning, are you? Try and I'll start talking about how I plan to redecorate this room and the Lincoln Bedroom and, come to think of it, the Roosevelt Room, which could use a sconce here, another sconce there, maybe a paint job. How are you with chartreuse?"

"Okay, no summit talk."

"And no decorating talk."

I read once or, more likely, watched a YouTube video about Barack Obama starting his day by talking about national security before he moved on to the economy before he moved onto something else important. I always liked Obama's understated sense of humor, and think he was joking. Obama probably saved the serious stuff until after he started his day by doing crossword puzzles or, like me, reading the sports page.

Other presidents, I've heard, started their day by tweeting. Other presidents started their day by reading the financial pages. One president, a buddy tells me, started off by looking in the mirror and reciting that old Stuart Smalley SNL bit: "I'm good enough, I'm smart enough and, doggone it, people like me."

Whatever works. For me, that means talking to Ariana. It's my premeditation meditation and gets me ready for a day talking about national security and economics, the summit and, damn it, infrastructure.

"Did you help Lin with her homework last night?" Ariana asks.

"Calculus? Are you kidding me? I'm going to pass a law outlawing calculus in the classroom. Besides, Lin is smarter than me."

"And going back to Northwestern next week."

"Yep. We'll be empty nesters."

"Except for the Secret Service."

I wish we had more time to talk this morning, but I'm meeting with my staff about the Jerusalem talks at 9. And I'll do my daily morning meditation before that.

Ariana pauses at the door before she leaves.

"And don't forget to take your meds."

"Yes, dear."

"You mean, yes FLOTUS,"

I love this woman.

I don't love my chances of getting the Israelis and Palestinians to stop killing each other long enough to accomplish something that never has existed -- peace in the Middle East -- but that's what I'll spend much of my day talking about with my Cabinet.

First, though, I'll meditate. Maybe I'll meditate twice.

CHAPTER 3

Gladys, as usual, is the first to arrive at the morning staff meeting. She has the notepads, the newspapers and even the coffee – decaf for my press secretary -- laid out so we can busy ourselves with the important stuff.

Actually, I think Gladys might be the most important person in this whole building. I can only imagine the fallout from press briefings if my press secretary was amped up on three cups of caffeinated coffee when she talked to reporters. Aida Manuel is good but tends to go off the cuff with news organizations dying to bring me down.

Tarik is the third to arrive, just after me. I've known Tarik since I was beating the crap out of him on the basketball court at Lea Elementary School. That's not why I made him my Chief of Staff, although it's nice not to get picked last when we have staff pickup games. Tarik made law review at Temple. I didn't. Tarik was the guy who got me elected mayor and then governor and then president. I might have had something to do with it – Ariana tells me I charm the crowds – but Tarik is the one who does the leg work, is the only one other than Ariana who has the balls to tell me when I'm full of shit and is one of the few who knows I am bipolar.

One other thing: Tarik is Black. As much as I'd like to think we live in a society where race doesn't matter, we don't. Optics matter. The fact that I have had an African American Chief of Staff through all of my campaigns has helped me have all of these campaigns, not just one failed mayoral race.

"The Jerusalem summit, guys, the summit," I start the meeting. "Where do we stand?"

Silence until Tarik speaks up.

"Actually, Mr. President, your question should be 'where do we sit?'" Tarik says. "The Israelis want a round table. Intifada wants a long, rectangular table, probably so they can sit as far away from the Israelis as possible. Personally, I want two poker tables. If we can't attain peace in the Middle East, at least I can win some money. I hear Farid Fadal is a lousy poker player."

"I know it's next to impossible for you, Tarik, but can you be serious for a second? We're talking about solving a problem that's lasted forever."

"Which is why I'm talking poker. Do you really think you'll fix something that can't be fixed?"

Tarik might have a point. I'm sure our week-long summit at nearby Camp David is not going to solve a blood feud that started well before Israel became a state in 1948 and has continued through wars, suicide bombings, Israeli settlements on the West Bank and former PLO leader Yasser Arafat winning a Nobel Peace Prize in 1994. I never understood that one. Who, exactly, was he competing against?

But this is a new day. Or so my advisors tell me. The Palestinian government, Intifada, has a charter that calls for the elimination of Israel. But it looks like Intifada– or at least it's leader, Farid Fadal -- might be coming around. If so, it's long overdue. Palestinians have suffered for far too long under Intifada and Fadal might realize that it's better to play nice with an Israeli army that could squash Gaza and the West Bank like bugs.

"I wouldn't trust him, Mr. President," Nasir Arwish, one of my Middle East advisors warns me for the umpteenth time. "Farid fought with Arafat. He lost his mother in the Six Day War, lost one of his wives in the Yom Kippur War. He's just playing you."

"Or maybe, just maybe, he doesn't want to lose another one of his wives," one of my other Middle East advisors, Aisha James, says. "As the late, great John Lennon said, let's give peace a chance."

"Peace?" Arwish says. "Even if Israel and Intifada agree, there's Nakbar ready to pounce in the north. And there's the head of the snake, Iran. Give peace a chance? John Lennon is turning over in his grave."

Farid's Israeli counterpart, Noah Abrams, also is saying the right things, talking about a two-state solution and the need for greater Palestinian representation in the Israeli government. But Abrams, who went to school in Philly before ditching cheesesteaks to become Israel's Prime Minister, keeps building settlements on the West Bank. And his right-hand man, Schlomo Glickstein, said on Israeli TV that Jordan, Egypt and "any Arab country that really cares about the Palestinians" should open their borders and "let them in." The microphones still were on when Glickstein, thinking they had gone to commercial, said "those Jew-haters wouldn't be our problem anymore."

And I think I can fix this? I know I have bipolar disorder. Maybe I have narcissistic personality disorder, too.

CHAPTER 4

Dr. Carty entered my life in 1987, about the 15th psychiatrist I saw after descending into the depths of my bipolar depression.

I know it was 1987 only because the Twins and Cardinals were involved in an epic World Series and I couldn't focus on it. I also couldn't focus on my family, my job or even taking a shower. People talk about the roller-coaster ride of people who live with bipolar disorder. My ride had one short peak – that night when I was crossing the Walnut Street Bridge – but the rest of my experience battling an illness that had me contemplating suicide was more like bumper cars. And I was the one crashing into deep depression.

My friend, Chris, recommended Dr. Carty after he helped one of Chris' friends climb out of her depression. What the heck, I thought. It's not like I was working – I had taken a leave of absence from the EEOC for "personal reasons" -- and had plenty of time for psychiatrist visits.

"Ahh, the good old days," I say to Dr. Carty as we start our bi-weekly session in a room in the basement of the White House. Dr. Carty moved his practice consisting of one patient – me – to D.C. shortly after I was elected president.

"Not so good for you. It's why you came to see me in the first place."

Dr. Carty certainly had presidential psychiatric credentials when I started seeing him, even though I was a long way from the Oval Office at the time. He was a Harvard graduate and had treated at least two Philly mayors and three governors before me.

Eric – we're on a first-name basis now – impressed me most with somebody he didn't treat. He knew Bonnie Raitt, who was going to all-female Radcliffe College when Eric was going to all-male Harvard. Eric went on to become the president's psychiatrist. Bonnie dropped out of Radcliffe and went on to sing some of the most beautiful ballads and ballsiest blues I ever heard. If we're measuring success, I give Bonnie the nod.

"First, have you been taking your meds?" Carty starts.

"You're all about the meds. What about the journaling, the mindfulness, the cardio exercises you turned me on to?"

"It looked like you were nodding off at your last press conference."

"There's your answer. Lithium makes you sleepy."

"Drink more coffee."

A lot of psychiatrists back when I was hopping from one to another felt differently than Eric.

"You have garden variety depression," one of them told me.

"It makes sense," another said. "You finished law school, you had some success early on and then you realized you didn't want to be a lawyer. It's a simple existential crisis you'll have to wait out with meds and a little patience."

They fed me anti-depressant after anti-depressant, and I didn't get better. In fact, I got worse because I lost hope with every med and every doctor. One of my uncles spent most of his adult life in a mental hospital before dying there. I wondered whether the same fate waited for me.

And then I started seeing Eric. Midway through our first session, Eric said I had been misdiagnosed. He said I had bipolar disorder, the same illness my uncle had, and prescribed lithium. He also told me to exercise, meditate and practice mindfulness.

I was feeling much better by the second appointment. I felt like the cloud that had darkened my life for nearly three years had lifted by our third appointment. My energy was back and my suicidal thoughts were gone. The little things that gave me no pleasure during my three-year period of darkness – a cup of coffee at the breakfast table, playing with my nephews – had returned.

"You're a genius," I told Eric.

"The genius is the guy who came up with lithium," he said. "I'm just the doctor who prescribed it."

I still use lithium over thirty years later while managing to get married, raise a beautiful daughter, win a mayoral election, win a gubernatorial election in the biggest landslide in Pennsylvania history and squeak by in a presidential election nobody thought I could win as an Independent.

If nodding off at an occasional press conference is the only side effect and that side effect can be countered with an extra cup of coffee, no problem. The public probably wouldn't be okay with it, though, which is why the only people who know about my bipolar are Ariana, Eric, Tarik, Lin and me.

"Have you been journaling lately?" Eric asks.

"Yep."

"Can I see what you've written?"

"I could show you, but I'd have to kill you. National security scribblings and all that."

"The meditation?"

"Every day."

"Your morning talks with Ariana?"

"Every morning, except when she's with the Secretary of State?"

Eric gasps.

"Want to talk about it?"

"No, because it doesn't happen. I was only joking."

Eric, like most people I meet these days, has changed a bit since I became president. He would have picked up on the joke a long time ago, although I would have substituted the mailman for the Secretary of State. I'm President now, but I haven't changed. I wish everybody viewed me that way.

I call my psychiatrist by his first name. I want Eric to call me by my first name, but he still slips and calls me Mr. President every now and then.

Still, he is my psychiatric anchor. And, despite my new-found status, Eric probably is the best chance I have of ever meeting my musical idol, Bonnie Raitt.

CHAPTER 5

Has there ever been an exciting infrastructure meeting? Give me a meeting with Noah Abrams and Farid Fadal any day of the week, but talking about infrastructure – does anybody outside the Beltway actually know what the word means? -- doesn't float my boat.

Which is why I practice my breathing exercises before I go into a meeting with Infrastructure Chief James Spearling. Which is why I will let one of my infrastructure experts do most of the talking with Spearling.

Which is why I have two cups of coffee before heading into a meeting I know is crucial for mass transit, telecommunications and the overall economy in this country. Still, infrastructure is boring as hell to me.

Spearling and his minions stand when I enter the room. They stand and applaud when I exit the room an hour later after I promise to pass the most comprehensive infrastructure bill in U.S. history.

My day is over except for dinner with Ariana and Lin.

"How was your meeting about the summit?" Ariana asks.

"We talked about furniture. I should have brought you along."

"And how was the infrastructure meeting?"

"About as exciting as listening to you talk about furniture."

"Now that you mention it, I'm thinking of putting a Zen fountain in the John Quincy Adams Room. Or should I go with a Moroccan motif? Or French Gothic?"

And Ariana is off to make dinner in the small kitchen we have in our quarters. The presidential chef is great – James Asher has cooked for four presidents – but Ariana wants to keep her hand in the game and has made my favorite tonight: lobster salad.

Which leaves me alone with Lin. We used to have a lot of alone time to talk about her studies and her continuing battle with social anxiety, but I just haven't had the time – or, maybe, I'm not making the time – since I became President.

"I got an A in calculus," Lin smiles.

"Figures. You're Chinese. And don't let anybody know I said that. It'll make me look like a bigot."

Lin knows I am joking. And she knows Ariana and I love her more than anything else in our lives. Especially more than infrastructure.

The best thing Ariana and I ever did since we married over twenty years ago was adopt Lin. China had a one-child policy which resulted in girls getting left on government steps. But we didn't do it for altruistic reasons. We did it because a friend had a good experience adopting from China and because Ariana and I desperately wanted a child after getting married so late in life.

I still remember the tears streaming down Ariana's face when she first held Lin in her arms in some nondescript government building in Nanchang. And I still remember changing Lin's diaper – she was an overachiever, even then – a few weeks later in a fancy Guangzhou hotel called the White Swan.

A few of my political rivals over the years tried to use the fact that we didn't go the domestic adoption route against me. Heart-tugging photos of baby Lin on cable news stations shut down the criticism.

"Your lobster salad, Mr. President," Ariana says, returning with a dish she made on our first date.

"Thank you, FLOTUS. Can you taste-test it first? I have enemies."

It's true. I do have enemies, which might include Abrams or Fadal or both. I'll find out next week.

Tonight, though, I'm with the people I love. It makes being President a little easier.

CHAPTER 6

The summit meeting room at Camp David is being outfitted – Tarik got his way with two poker tables, although they'll be used for negotiations and not Texas Hold 'Em – and I'm unusually calm.

Maybe it's low expectations. These guys have been going at it forever. What's a wannabe' hooper from West Philly supposed to do to fix it? Maybe it's the lithium. I take it for bipolar, but it helps with anxiety. I don't find myself flying off the handle when the Sixers commit inevitable turnovers that cost them playoff series anymore. Or, today, I don't feel anxious going into negotiations that could be the crowning achievement of my presidency if things work out right.

Or maybe it's the five secret service agents who will stand nearby while I try to keep Noah and Farid from engaging in a food or knife fight.

Farid Fadal and his crew are the first to arrive at Camp David a week later. There are four sheiks with him, which gets me thinking about milkshakes – I've sworn off; bad for my cholesterol – and telling milk shake/sheik jokes.

But I don't speak Arabic and am sure the jokes would get lost in my translator's translation.

"Mr. President," Farid, who graduated from Harvard and speaks perfect English, says. "I trust that our summit will be fruitful. And all thanks to you – and to Allah – for arranging it."

"I get first billing over Allah? I am flattered."

I'm sitting across from a guy who used to be the head of the PLO, which trafficked in terror, whose suicide bombers took out Israeli women, children and anybody else in the vicinity when PLO "warriors" detonated bombs, killed themselves and went to virgin heaven.

I have to remind myself of that.

But I also have to remind myself that Fadal has buried a mother and a daughter killed in this ongoing conflict. I have to remind myself that Fadal, more so than Abrams, pushed for this summit. I have to remind myself that people can change and that change would behoove Gazans whose suffering has grown in recent years.

And one more thing: Fadal is up for reelection. He wants to stay on top, which makes him no different than any American politician.

"And how is the First Lady? Fadal asks. "Will she be making an appearance?"

"Thank you for asking. She is fine. But Ariana figured I'd have enough on my plate without having to worry about giving her back rubs. And how is your wife?"

"Wives. I trust you have expansive living quarters."

"I do. Hopefully, expansive enough to prevent arguments."

"I don't allow them to argue."

Another reason I'm glad Ariana stayed at the White House. She bristles at the fact that Fadal's faith allows him to have more than one wife even when I tell her that two wives are better than one and three are better than two.

She also bristles at the burkas, the fact that women don't have a vote, can't serve in government and, basically, are second-class citizens in Fadal's world. She thinks I'm only trying to humor her when she goes off on one of her female equality tangents, but I agree with everything she says.

"And when is Prime Minister Abrams arriving?" Fadal asks.

"Tomorrow. He's been to Washington. He wanted you to get here first."

"Just like we were first in Palestine."

"I assume he would disagree, but let's save it for the summit. For now, my chef has prepared a delicious shawarma, lamb kabob and tabbouleh dinner."

"I was praying for steak," Fadal says.

"He made that, too."

CHAPTER 7

To say that I knew Noah Abrams well when we were seniors at Central High in Philly would be a stretch. Oh, we went to the same school. But we ran in different circles, me with the "cool kids" who played sports and acted like all the girls were dying to sleep with us and Noah with the "Central nerds" who went from class presidents to, in Noah's case, Prime Minister of Israel.

I do remember one interaction with Noah, though. We were ready to play a pickup basketball game when I noticed Noah, forlorn, standing on the sidelines because, as usual, he hadn't been picked. I don't know if I was just trying to be nice or because my knee was bothering me, but I gave Noah my spot.

"Thanks," Noah said as he took the court. "I'll help you with your homework."

Noah wasn't so thankful after he missed all of his shots, committed at least 10 turnovers and was almost solely responsible for his team's loss. I never saw him at the basketball court again and we rarely spoke even when I beat him for class president in our senior year.

PNT, DVTV, the New York Beacon, the Washington Guardian and just about all of the mainstream media have written stories embellishing my relationship with Noah, calling us "best friends" and wondering how I could be fair to the Palestinians during the summit because I was "so close" to Noah.

If only they knew.

"You know," Noah says when he and his right-hand man, Schlomo Glickstein, arrive the next day and we meet in the Camp David conference room, "you didn't do me any favors by letting me play in that game."

"And you never helped me with my homework."

"I hope you did your homework for our meeting with the Palestinians. I have broken the news to too many Israeli mothers after their children died in suicide bombings. I don't want to do it again."

"Our interests align. I don't want more Israeli deaths. I don't want more Palestinian deaths. And, if I can juggle three balls at once, I also want to do what is best for my country."

"It's worth a shot, something I didn't make in that basketball game."

Noah smiles for the first time since we shook hands to start the meeting. Good.

"A long shot," he adds.

Bad.

Later, we gather around the large, round negotiating table. One of my favorite Curb Your Enthusiasm episodes is when Larry David riffs on the importance of seating arrangements. When Larry and Susie nail the seating arrangement in the episode, Susie's meticulously planned dinner goes well.

Farid, the various sheiks and their translator are seated on one side of the table. Noah, Schlomo and his translator are seated across from the Palestinian contingent. Normally, I would sit at the head of the table, but there are no heads of tables when the tables are round.

"Tea, anyone?" It's Martha. She handles the culinary pleasantries when I meat with heads of state at Camp David.

"Chamomile, please," Farid says. "If you have it."

"Of course we have it," I say. "At least that's what CIA intelligence tells me."

Farid laughs. Noah doesn't.

"Coffee," Noah says. "Black."

With seating arrangements and tea/coffee preferences out of the way, it's on to business. But not before I deliver an opening statement.

"Gentlemen, I brought you here to at least make inroads toward a lasting peace. Presidents before me have failed and I have no illusions. But I know, Farid, that you want what is best for your people and Noah, I know that you want what is best for your people."

"And you, Mr. President, want what is best for your people," Noah interrupts. "And you have an election coming up. It would be best for you, too."

Noah is right. Success at Camp David will help me. But that is not why I scheduled this summit. My people on the ground tell me that the Palestinians, for the first time since the Oslo Accords, want peace. They also tell me that Noah's popularity in Israel is waning and that success at the summit could propel him to another term.

Peace in the Middle East still is a long shot. But it's better than no shot.

"Can I say something before we delve into the important matters?" Farid asks.

"Surely."

Farid turns toward Noah, who shifts uncomfortably in his seat.

"We have had our differences over the years, Mr. Prime Minister. Your people have suffered. My people have suffered. It is my sincere hope that we can end the suffering. You have been a worthy opponent, but I do not want you to be an opponent. I want you to be an ally, although I know that will not happen. I will settle for a peaceful coexistence."

Noah looks like he is waiting for a punchline but gets something quite different.

"Shalom aleichem," Farid says.

I don't need a translator to tell me that it means peace be unto you.

I also know from dealing with enough Arab diplomats that the appropriate response is "aleichem, shalom."

Instead: "More coffee," Noah says. "Can we please get started?"

CHAPTER 8

It is an unseasonably warm February day in the Camp David courtyard the following afternoon, made even warmer by Farid Fadal and Noah Abrams.

"Peace in the Middle East," Farid declares, smiling and bowing in the direction of Abrams. "Unless President Pappas wants me as a permanent guest at Camp David, I am not leaving without it."

Noah – the competitor in my old Central classmate coming out – manages an almost imperceptible bow.

"Actions, President Fadal, speak louder than words,"

And then we go inside, PNT, DVTV and all of the news outlets having gotten what they came for: photos that surely will boost ratings and provide fodder for all of the talking heads employed by all of the talking head stations.

Farid goes to his quarters to pray.

Noah retreats to his quarters, telling us that he must speak to his advisor, Schlomo Glickstein.

And we meet in the conference room an hour later: Farid, the sheiks, Abrams, Glickstein, Tarik and me. I'm encouraged after listening to Farid and Noah speak to the press. Maybe we really can make history here.

Or not.

"Ah, yes, peace in the Middle East," Noah starts. "It really is a noble aspiration, President Fadal. If only you meant it."

"I do mean it."

"Tell that to the suicide bomber who, my adviser tells me, just killed 57 people in a Tel Aviv coffee house. Oh, wait. You can't tell him. He's dead, having fulfilled his duty to Allah or whoever it is he was taking orders from."

Thank God – Allah or otherwise – there aren't any TV cameras capturing what I hoped would be a productive start to the conference.

"We can end the conference now, Prime Minster Abrams, if you think I had anything to do with it."

Farid whispers to one of the sheiks, who hustles out of the room.

"You expect me to believe..." Abrams begins.

"I *hope* you believe, but I don't expect anything. I am telling you the truth. I may be the leader of Intifada, but I do not control everything my people do, just as I am sure all Israelis do not do what you want them to do."

"Gentlemen, gentlemen." Thank God – Allah or otherwise – for Martha. A woman who probably will write a New York Beacon bestseller when she stops working for me, has been waiting for the right time to bring coffee to Abrams and tea to Farid.

More importantly, she gives the combatants a chance to cool off.

"I will be drinking my coffee in my room" Abrams says.

"And I will be having tea – and praying yet again – in mine," Farid says.

"We'll meet back here in an hour," I say.

I get no answer as Farid, the various sheiks, Abrams and Glickstein leave the room.

Which leaves Tarik, Martha and me.

"Remind me to give you a raise," I tell Martha.

"Give me a raise."

"Remind me again some other time."

Martha leaves and Tarik gives me the stare he gave me back at Lea School when I didn't listen to him and was suspended for sticking a tack on a teacher's chair. It's the stare he gave me when I asked a woman whose name

I forget but whose profession – she was a stripper – to marry me over 40 years ago when I was drunk in a West Philly club. It's the stare he has given me countless times throughout my political career, most recently when I told him of my plans to hold this summit.

Tarik doesn't need to say, "I told you so." The Lea School stare says it all.

"We'll hash things out when they come back," I say.

"If they come back."

CHAPTER 9

I'm sitting in the conference room alone two hours later and all I hear is Mom's voice over and over and over again: *"Time will tell. Time will tell. Time will tell."*

My Mom was the Greek Buddha and would have made a great religious leader if she wasn't so busy raising me and my two sisters. She had a million sayings and would hit me with at least one of them – annoyingly so -- every time we got together. I didn't like it much then, but would give anything to hear my Mom, who died five years ago, today.

Time is telling me now that this whole summit idea is a bust. My intentions weren't purely altruistic – I have an election to win sometime in the future – but I really thought we could make some kind of progress. The press will have a field day with a summit that didn't last a full day. Even worse, I expect tensions in the Middle East to increase after this latest attack.

Which is when Farid walks in, followed a few minutes later by Noah. Time will tell? I'm more interested in what my two guests will tell.

"It was Islamic Jihad," Farid says after everyone takes their place at the table. "An Islamic Jihad terrorist trying to end this summit before it begins. They don't want peace. They want power. And Israeli deaths."

I look to Noah, who is sipping his coffee. But it's his advisor, ultra-right wing Schlomo Glickstein, who speaks up.

"You know I was against this summit, President Fadal. And you know I feel that peace in the Middle East, a real peace, is impossible. But – and our intelligence service confirms this – it was Islamic Jihad Not that I expect anything to come out of this conference, but we should continue."

"We never really started," I say, putting on my best poker face while turning cartwheels inside. "More coffee or tea before we start, anyone?"

"No," Noah says. "We already have wasted too much time."

First on the agenda are Israeli settlements on the West Bank. Settlements have increased three-fold under Noah's leadership, displacing Palestinians, leading to increased violence and drawing the ire of an international community which has almost universally condemned the settlements as a violation of international law.

Farid wants Noah to abandon any settlements made within the last two years. Noah wants to increase settlements, "as a hedge against violence directed toward the Israeli people."

"Is there a middle ground here?" I ask.

"No." It took Noah about a tenth of a second to respond.

"Absolutely not." It took Farid two-tenths of a second to respond.

"There are other issues," I say. "Perhaps we can find tradeoffs."

Farid and Noah are silent. I take that as a mini victory.

Next up are attacks on Israelis, most in Gaza but a number committed by suicide bombers in Israel who have claimed thousands of lives.

"This is untenable," Noah says. "You want more rights, maybe even your own state, how can Israelis be confident that these attacks will not increase if we cede power?"

"You can't be confident now," Farid responds. "But I am doing my best. I was the only member of the Intifada council pushing for peace when I took over. Now, although most of the council still condones these attacks, more of my countrymen feel like I do."

"It might help if you take, 'Death to Israel,' out of your Constitution," Noah says.

"I agree, Mr. Prime Minister."

Ariana wanted me to talk about the lack of women's and gay rights in Palestine, but I'm not going there. Not yet. Farid and Noah seem amenable to settlement talk and deescalating the violence, and I don't want to inject another matter that, no doubt, Palestine will view as the U.S. trying to impose its morality on a foreign country.

We discuss Palestinian representation in the Knesset and Israel's control of water rights to Gaza and the West Bank. I also broach the subject of Israel possibly returning land it won in the Six-Day War.

"That," Noah says, "is a non-starter."

"So, we won't start it," Farid smiles. "I believe we should break for the day?"

It is 8 p.m. We have been going at this non-stop for seven hours and I am sure a dinner with Noah, Farid, the sheiks, Glicksten and Tarik would take the edge off.

"With all due respect, Mr. President," Farid says. "I don't want to dine with you."

What?

"I want to dine with Prime Minister Abrams."

What?

"I agree," Abrams says. "And don't worry. We will not kill each other. But I cannot promise that we will not throw food."

CHAPTER 10

Normally, I like to stand front and center when the media snaps photos of me meeting with diplomats, championship basketball teams, pretty much anything. And it's not an ego thing. Okay, maybe it is partly an ego thing, but I also want to exude strength and let the American people know who is in charge.

And there's something else: I want people to vote for me. Can't have a third-string center on the team that won the NBA championship stealing my spotlight.

I gladly let Farid and Noah take center stage the rest of the week, though. After their dinner that first night, they act like friends the rest of the conference or as close to friends as Israeli and Palestinian leaders can act after a blood feud that has lasted for well over a century.

"I was wrong," Tarik tells me as we wait for Noah and Farid to make their way to the conference room for our last day of talks.

"Too loud in here. I missed what you said."

"I was wrong. This conference has been much more productive than I expected."

"Can you repeat that?"

"*Much* more productive."

"I was going for the 'I was wrong' part."

The issue of Israeli settlements on the West Bank was a no-go at the beginning of the conference. But, after some tense negotiations, Farid and

Noah have tied Israeli settlements into attacks on Israel. No more settlements, Noah promised, as long as there are no more attacks. If a year passes with no more attacks, Abrams promised Farid, he might consider relocating two settlements.

The "death to Israel" portion of the Intifada constitution? Farid promised to amend the constitution by presidential fiat when he returned home. Israel's control of water rights to Gaza and the West Bank? Abrams promised to give Palestinians a role, if not an equal role, in the flow of water.

Abrams stopped short -- well short -- of promising to return land Israel won in the Six-Day War.

"For the protection of my people," he said.

"And if your people no longer are in danger, which will be my primary goal as Intifada leader?"

"Finders keepers, losers weepers?" Noah smiled.

He didn't get any laughs for an expression he no doubt picked up when he lived in the U.S. And he only got a mild laugh after he explained to Farid that it meant Israel won the war and was entitled to keep the land.

"You could have said, 'To the victor goes the spoils,' " Farid said.

"Not as catchy."

I didn't expect a yuk-fest when we started this conference, but it looks like Farid and Noah have established a genuine bond by the end of the week. Of course, they could be making nice for the cameras. They have elections to win, too. If peace in the Middle East doesn't fly with their constituents, I could see Israeli – Palestinian tensions returning to blood-sport levels.

But I'm buoyed when the summit ends. More than buoyed. I'm feeling a high I haven't felt since the Eagles won the Super Bowl in 2018.

"A high, huh?" Ariana says when we go to bed on my first night back at the White House. "Did you take your meds?"

"I'll go down in history as the American president who brought peace to the Middle East, who accomplished something nobody said could be done, who is the Abraham Lincoln of our time, except better looking."

"You didn't take your meds."

"No."

"If you think you're getting any tonight, you are mistaken. Unless you take your meds. One more manic episode, the kind we covered up when you were Governor, and you're a one-term President."

I take my meds. I want to be more than a one-term President. I also want to cuddle with my wife.

CHAPTER 11

The New York Beacon hails the summit as "a huge success" and "President Pappas' finest hour" the next day. I just wish the paper didn't sprinkle the front page with 13 other stories, used bigger print on my story and had more pictures.

The Washington Guardian did have more pictures, although there was only one of me. Farid and Noah stole my spotlight, although I'll be sure to steal it back in my seventh – and possibly last – State of the Union address next week.

PNT's Jack Tanner, a Philly boy who always has been in my corner: "If this doesn't get President Pappas elected for a second term, I don't know what will."

DVTV's Bekka Mornay, who usually is in my corner except when I'm not liberal enough for her taste: "Farid and Abrams may be on the verge of striking a deal that Israelis and Palestinians have been yearning for. And the world has President Pappas to thank for it." All good, except Mornay has an annoying tendency to pontificate before she gets to the point of her stories and didn't mention me until 20 minutes into her opening monologue. Maybe I wasn't her point, Ariana tells me.

VOX's Brolin Murphy has called me "a snowflake," "a liberal snowflake in Independent clothing" and – my favorite -- "a buffoon." He couldn't quite bring himself to compliment me. "A broken clock," Murphy says, "is right twice a day." I'd like to clean Murphy's clock and I'm planning, as the first

Independent to occupy the White House, to clean the clocks of anybody the Democrats and Republicans send my way in November.

"I'd keep the cleaning clock thing to myself," Ariana says as we finish breakfast and prepare to go off to our respective jobs.

"I thought I did keep it to myself."

"No. You said it out loud. Just now. Are you sure you took your meds last night."

"As sure as I am about my mythic love for you."

"Save the bullshit for your State of the Union."

Ariana is off to meet with the director of Planned Parenthood. My wife is firmly pro-choice but has a problem with Planned Parenthood's image as an abortion factory. She wants to talk image to Sandra Eckhardt while not diluting Planned Parenthood's policies.

Other First Ladies have busied themselves with the Rose Garden and decorating the White House. I'd be wasting Ariana's talents if I didn't use her for more, so I usually ask her to deal with women's issues and the result has been a number of pro-woman bills which might not have passed if there was a point man and not a point woman.

I am discussing the State of the Union address later with Jim Banoff, the best speech writer I have had during my long political career. He is dramatic, but not overly so. He is funny, but not as funny as me and I'll often substitute one of my lines for his. And he isn't cliched, which is pretty much all you hear when a politician opens his mouth.

"We'll hit them up front with Israel-Palestine," Jim says when we meet in the Oval Office. "And make sure you mention Farid and Abrams more than you mention yourself. You don't want to come across as too self-aggrandizing."

"Self-aggrandizing is what I do. Please?"

"Do you want to get re-elected?"

I file this under the "changeable" portion of the speech. We had a president in the non-so-distant pass who was so-so on policy but big on promoting himself through endless tweeting. He was elected to serve a second term. I want to be elected again, too, and – although I disagreed with many of that president's policies – I admired how he pretty much rode his charisma into the White House.

"And save gun control for last," Banoff warns as we wrap up our meeting. "It's a hot-button issue and you don't want to risk alienating all of the gun advocates who liked what you did at the summit."

"Even with that school shooting last week?"

"*Do* something about gun control. Just don't *say* much about it or save it for the late in the speech after you've put the older Republican and Democratic senators to sleep."

And Jim is off to work on his first draft of his speech, while I'm off to my weekly one-on-one basketball game with Tarik on a court I started building the first day I moved into the White House.

CHAPTER 12

I can see them, but they can't see me.

There's Trey Collins, sitting on the right chatting up his Republican buddies. Unless Collins is caught having sex with an armadillo or, worse, voting for safer gun laws, he will be the Republican nominee for President.

And there's Griffin Johnston, the presumptive presidential nominee for the Democrats. Collins is moving from row to row on the Republican side of the room, gladhanding anybody in the way. Johnston isn't moving because he has arthritis, is 79 years old and people come to him. He was my role model when I was considering a run for President. I still like the guy, but he clearly isn't as sharp as he was when he was taking down conservative nominees to the Supreme Court with rapier-like cross-examination.

And there's Lin and Ariana. They don't have a section for Independents, so they are sitting off-stage, not far from where I will deliver my State of the Union message. But they aren't truly Independent. I'm pretty sure I have their votes.

"You ready, brother?" Tarik says, reaching for a cigarette in the Green Room.

"I thought you quit."

"I was going to give it to you. Isn't that what they do when someone goes in front of a firing squad?"

"Way to boost my confidence, buddy."

"No problem."

We hug. I love this guy.

I see Ariana and Lin shifting in their seats, I see Collins still jabbering away and I see Democrats still lining up for the privilege of kissing Griffin Johnston's ring.

I also hear Speaker of the House Patricia Paschall, who has been around nearly as long as Johnston, addressing Congress.

"And now, the President of the United States."

Ariana dressed me. I was pushing for my Eagles green jacket, but she made me wear red, white and blue. Boring. Hopefully, I won't bore everybody with what I am about to say.

"Thank you, thank you," I start after I walk to the dais, motioning for everybody to sit down and hoping they remain standing and cheering. "You want to get out of here soon, I'd cut the ovation short. I hear they're running Godfather I and Godfather II back-to-back on TNT."

Banoff is shaking his head stage right. That wasn't on the teleprompter. What? I'm not allowed to have fun just because I'm President?

"Thank you, Patricia, for the introduction and for the outstanding work you've done as Speaker," I start. "And thank you, Senators Johnston and Collins, for cutting into your campaign schedule. I haven't had a chance to campaign yet, unless you want to consider my address tonight in front of 100 million people the beginning of my campaign. Have you ever addressed 100 million people at once, Trey? Griffin? Maybe you will someday. Four years from now."

Laughs from both sides of the aisle. Collins even manages to crack a smile.

"This is a beginning of sorts. Over the last few weeks, as you know, I have met with the Prime Minister of Israel and the President of Palestine in an effort to bring us closer to peace to the Middle East. Many people in the press, in this room – even in my Cabinet – warned against it. It'll blow up in your face, I was told. Many presidents have tried and failed. What makes you think you're so different?

"Well, I'm not different. All of the presidents before me were in the same position I'm in: leader of the most powerful country in the world. And all of those presidents, no doubt, sought to use their power to end the longest – and one of the bloodiest – wars this world has ever known.

"Here is the difference. Farid Fadal, the Palestinian leader, truly wants peace. I really believe that. And Noah Abrams, prime minister of our greatest ally, Israel, wants peace, too. To the extent you can attain peace in two weeks where none has existed for centuries, we did that. We had productive talks on Israeli settlements on the West Bank, Islamic Jihad attacks on Israelis and many other issues.

I glance over at Banoff, who is smiling ear to ear because I have not strayed from his script after my initial remarks.

"Of course, I hope I am standing in front of you next year at this time talking about a lasting peace that had its genesis at Camp David. But if one of my competitors – Senators Johnston, Collins or someone else – is standing here, I will be just as happy if we have lasting peace."

I almost believe what I just said.

"But we don't have to look only at the Middle East to be optimistic. We can look at this great country of ours. The economy is booming. Race relations have improved since I signed House Bill 332, but we have a long way to go. We have a very long way to go on safe gun control laws, but we'll get there. We'll get there because we all love America. We'll get there because we all love the prospect of what America can be."

Banoff looks stunned. I have not strayed from his script for one of the few times – the only time? -- in my presidency.

"God bless you, everybody in this hallowed hall. And God bless

America. Thank you."

I walk offstage with Ariana and Lin. I am the one who is blessed.

And I walk straight into a Tarik bear hug.

"You were great," he says.

"You smell like cigarettes."

"Nerves. I didn't think you'd be great."

CHAPTER 13

Ariana tells me the next morning that she was surprised I squeezed through the White House door the previous night.

"All those people cheering for you, all that love," Ariana says. "Don't they know your head swells to the size of the Goodyear blimp every time somebody smiles at you, let alone when you get standing ovations?"

"Maybe they're trying to send me into manic mode again. That way, Johnston and Collins won't have to run against the greatest president since Abraham Lincoln. By the way, I thought Daniel Day Lewis played a great Lincoln in the movie. Who do you think should play me?"

"Jack Nicholson. He got an Oscar for *One Flew Over the Cuckoo's Nest.* Which reminds me, did you take your meds last night?"

"Of course."

I hate it when I lie to Ariana. I got caught up in the post-State of the Union hoopla and forgot. I'll double up on the dosage today, although I'm not sure if you're supposed to double up.

If Ariana thinks I was insufferable last night, she'll probably file for divorce when I get back from the Oval Office today.

Tarik and I are watching TV later, popcorn and chocolate-covered Raisinets on the table, as reporters try to out-gush each other.

VOX is the most subdued, but Brett Bishop looks like he is inching closer to joining the Evan Pappas fan club. "Just be glad, Republicans, that he's running as an Independent. The last time was a fluke. He runs against

Collins as a Democrat and we can kiss the next four years goodbye."

"Would you run as a Democrat?" Tarik asks.

"Nope. I believe what I believe and don't want a party – Democrat or Republican – telling me what I'm supposed to do."

"Sounds like commitment problems to me."

"It's not about commitment problems. It's about wanting to be my own man."

"Sounds like denial problems to me."

A new reporter is salivating over my performance on PNT. I don't know her name, but it looks like PNT is starting to follow the VOX model: she is young, pretty and, as an added bonus, smart. "He was funny, he hit all the right notes and he had plenty of material to work with. The Israel – Palestine summit might be the crowning achievement for any president this century."

"Who is she?" Tarik says.

"Beats me, but can you have your people get in touch with PNT's people and ask them to give her a raise?"

"If my people get in touch with PNT's people, it will be to get her phone number."

"Inappropriate."

"I'd only do it to help you in the polls."

And, finally, there is Bekka Mornay, working double-duty on DVTV. She was on last night, is on this morning, and still hasn't said my name 40 minutes into her opening monologue.

I turn off the TV before Bekka gets to the good part, assuming there is a good part.

"Do you have time for a quick game of one-on-one?" Tarik asks.

"Can't. Have to get ready for the gun control town hall and, before that, I have an appointment with Dr. Carty."

"Make sure you talk to him about those commitment issues. Running as a Democrat or Republican, if either side asks, would give you a better shot at a second term."

"It also would give you better shot at job security."

"Bingo."

CHAPTER 14

D r. Carty is listening to Mozart when I enter his office for a meeting I had to cancel when I was in Camp David.

"I didn't know you were a classical musical guy," I say.

"Mozart, yes. Most classical music, no. Plus, psychiatrists are supposed to maintain an air of sophistication. I can't let you hear me listening to what I really love – death metal – when we meet."

"Death metal? Seriously?"

"Not seriously. You're losing your sense of humor, Evan. All of this saving the world stuff is going to your head."

I used to think Eric engaged in small talk at the beginning of our sessions to eat up part of our hour together. Then, I thought it was because he wanted to ease me into the real stuff. Now, I know that it's just Eric being Eric, the way he wants me to be me and not President of the United States.

Ariana knows me better than anyone, but Eric is a close second.

"I caught your State of the Union last night," he says.

"And did you love it as much as PNT, DVTV, VOX, pretty much all of the fawning media who are doing their best to get me elected to a second term?"

"Actually, no. It looked like you were about to go full-blown manic in front of 100 million viewers."

I have no idea what he is talking about. I felt fine. Everybody I've talked to thought I was fine, although most of the people I talk to tell me what they think I want to hear. Ariana is an exception. Lin is becoming an exception, making me long sometimes for her younger years when everything was, "Yes, Daddy. You're right, Daddy."

"What makes you say that? You're the only one."

"I'm your only psychiatrist."

Eric tells me that I have a tell. In poker, that's a bad thing. You lose money when somebody spots it. In politics, it's worse if the tell blossoms into a mental meltdown.

"It wasn't anything you said. It was the way you moved. You were fidgeting, and you never fidget. You were blinking way too much, and you rarely blink. Your speech, it seemed pressured."

"And you noticed all of this from the comfort of your living room."

"I noticed it from a bar. Being psychiatrist to the leader of the free world is no picnic. I had a couple shots, a few burgers and danced with my wife when they played "Crazy." Patsy Cline was my favorite until Bonnie Raitt came along. Overall, a good night except when I watched you."

I felt great coming into this session. I don't feel so great now.

"But it's nothing you can't fix," Eric says. "Just keep taking your meds."

"Ummm..."

"You're not taking your meds?"

"Not last night. And a couple of nights during the summit."

I've never seen Eric pissed, really pissed. But he is pissed now. At least, I think he is pissed when he takes Mozart off the turntable, replaces it by a group that probably is named "Suicide" or "Megadeath" and turns up the volume.

"Make it stop!" I say.

"This is what your brain will sound like if you stop taking your meds. You talk about peace in the Middle East. How about peace of mind. You lose it and everything falls apart."

He's right. I've been full of myself lately, with the summit talks and my State of the Union and a presidential election which I'm sure I'll win in a landslide.

I'm sure I'll win in a landslide? Damn, I really am full of myself.

"I'll take my meds. And I'll practice mindfulness every day, something else I've been bad at lately, too."

"Good," Eric says. "Now, I can go back to Mozart."

CHAPTER 15

The Gun Control Town Hall tonight is set up differently than town halls I have participated in or watched in the past.

PNT is broadcasting it. Brolin Murphy from VOX is fielding questions from the pro-gun people sitting on the right side of the room. Bekka Mornay from DVTV is fielding questions from the gun control people on the left side of the room. I just hope she lets the people talk and doesn't launch into one of her patented monologues.

"Thank you all for joining in on our conversation about guns," I tell the audience at the outset. "Notice that I said 'conversation.' Too often, these things turn into shouting matches which do nothing to accomplish what we all want: fair gun laws that lead to safer streets. Tonight, though, we're going to have a conversation with each other. And if anybody tries to turn this into a shouting match, you will be escorted from the room. And that includes you, Brolin. And you, Bekka."

A couple of chuckles from the crowd. I thought the joke deserved more.

I don't tell the audience that I got the idea for the structure of this town hall from group therapy. Dr. Carty suggested that I join a bipolar group after I experienced my first manic episode decades ago and it worked wonders for my mental health.

And I don't tell Mornay or Murphy that I look at them as my 'co-facilitators.' That's what the therapists who ran my group called themselves, wanting to put the emphasis on facilitating, not leading. I might be President of the United States, but I want to facilitate this group, not lead it. I expect Murphy and Mornay to follow suit.

The person who takes the microphone first, from Murphy's side of the room, doesn't stick with the script.

"How the hell do you liberal snowflakes sitting over there expect me to protect myself?" Jack from Kokomo, Indiana yells at audience members on the other side of the room.

One of my Secret Service agents escorts Jack from the town hall shortly thereafter.

"Like I said, people," I say after calm is restored. "We're going to have a conversation with each other, not a shouting match. Who's next?"

It's Sally from New York City.

"Snowflakes don't kill people," Sally smirks toward the pro-gun crowd. "Guns, especially if they're in the hands of right-wing fascists like you guys, do."

Sally gets a quick exit, too.

"Listen, guys," I say. "I'm a politician. And politicians love to talk. If you want, I can take up the rest of the hour talking both sides of the issue, throwing out a couple of high-sounding campaign promises and promoting my new book, soon to be in bookstores near you at an unbelievably reasonable price. Do you really want that?"

"If I may interject, Mr. President," Mornay says.

"No, you may not, Bekka. But one of the people from your side of the room can."

It's Gene from Portland, Oregon.

"I'm anti-gun, but I get that we need to protect our loved ones. And having a gun in the house for self-protection might not be a bad idea."

You go, Gene.

And then there is Elvis from Little Rock, Arkansas on Brolin's side of the room.

"My daughter died in that mass shooting in Little Rock last year," he says. "Last thing I want is some lunatic packing an AK-47 entering a school building. But please don't take away my Second Amendment rights."

"Sorry for your loss, Elvis," Gene from Portland says.

"Thank you."

This is more like it. Pro-gun people talking to anti-gun people without me saying a word. But I can't help myself.

"I echo Gene's sentiments and, I'm sure, the sentiments of everyone here," I tell Elvis. "I have a daughter of my own and cringe to think of what could happen to her if we don't solve this problem. Piggybacking on your statement, Elvis, can I have a show of hands of people in favor of AK-47s?"

Not a single hand.

"See, guys," I say, "you have more in common than you think. How about having metal detectors at all schools?"

It's about 50-50 on this one, the split close to equal on both sides.

"This is going better than I expected, guys," I say. "Anybody want to join hands and sing "Kumbaya?""

Most get the joke and laugh but a couple of people – again split equally on both sides of the room – start singing.

I feel high, but not manic high after the rest of the Town Hall goes smoothly. Maybe we can pass meaningful gun legislation if Congress starts paying attention to the people who elected them and not the gun lobbies that finance their campaigns. Maybe I'll ask Dr. Carty to co-facilitate a joint session of Congress.

But my high vanishes when I see Tarik's ashen face in the hallway.

"There was a shooting," he says. "Sixteen dead at Ezekiel Baptist in Birmingham."

CHAPTER 16

How far have we come? How far have we fucking come since 1963 when a bomb at the 16th Street Baptist Church in Birmingham, a mile from Ezekiel Baptist, killed four Black girls and injured 10 others?

I think we've come a long way. The Civil Rights Act of 1964 and the Voting Rights Act of 1965 put African Americans on a more equal footing with Whites. Heck, we elected an African American President, something my grandparents wouldn't have wanted, and my parents only tolerated.

But I'm a White man. I watched African Americans cheering the O.J. verdict while Whites mourned. One of my Black friends cheered even though he thought O.J. was guilty. "This isn't about O.J.," he told me. "It's about us finally coming out on top."

There were riots early in my presidency after a Black man was killed by a policeman in Oshkosh. Republicans wanted me to impose martial law. Democrats wanted me to empathize with African Americans who had been beaten down so long, even as Black-owned businesses burned to the ground during the riots.

We held countless town balls about race, politicians made a lot of political hay and people who benefit from racial tension – the race hustlers on TV and some politicians– made a lot of money telling their constituents that this country hasn't progressed a lick since that Birmingham bombing in 1963.

I disagree. Then again, Air Force One is going to touch down in Birmingham in an hour to discuss 16 people murdered at Ezekiel Baptist.

"Do you think we've made progress?" I ask Tarik as we sit at the back of the plane.

"Of course. Why else would I have this job? Unless you just want somebody around you can beat in one-on-one."

"Seriously."

Tarik goes on to tell me that his parents and grandparents were victims of discrimination. Otherwise, he says, he wouldn't have been the first in the family to graduate from law school, let alone college.

He reminds me of the time Tarik, Prentice, me and Rick were playing two-on-two when we visited Rick in his lily-white suburban neighborhood. A car drove by the court, with one yahoo leaning out the window and shouting, "Niggers!" They got four middle fingers in return, and we went back to playing basketball: the brothers (Tarik and Prentice) against the others (Rick and I).

We didn't notice a group of 20-30 Whites walking down the hill minutes later to ring the court. Nothing happened to Rick and me. Tarik and Prentice got pushed around and the leader of the group told us to, "Go back where you came from."

Plus, I am President after getting elected Mayor of Philadelphia and Governor of Pennsylvania. Tarik hasn't complained about playing second fiddle to me once and I never gave it much thought.

Until now.

"I was the one who graduated cum laude from law school," Tarik says. "I was the one who won three straight moot court competitions while you read cliff notes to get by."

"I was the charming one," I smile.

"Fuck you, buddy."

We don't talk the rest of the trip until we're ready to touch down.

"I'm sorry," Tarik says. "I love my job. I love watching what you've done."

"What *we've* done. I'm the one who should be sorry. I haven't been paying attention."

We land, a number of reporters wait on the tarmac, and I have no idea what I am going to say to them or civic leaders I will meet in Birmingham.

"Just pay attention, Evan," Tarik says. "Just pay attention."

CHAPTER 17

Reverend Adolphus Jones' grandfather, John, marched with Dr. King in Selma and was one of the leading Black voices in the South for over three decades. He was jailed multiple times for protesting busing, housing and education issues, led one of the largest Black congregations in the entire South and was affectionately called "Saint Troublemaker" by his parishioners.

Like Dr. King, he preached non-violence.

Like Dr. King, he put his life on the line against attack dogs, attack Whites and sheriffs who answered his nonviolence with clubs and firehoses.

And, like Dr. King, he was assassinated.

I am meeting with Reverend Adolphus Jones today at the downtown Hilton because the place where we should be meeting – Lewis' Ezekiel Baptist church – was burned to the ground after the shooter took out 16 parishioners.

"You know what my grandfather told me when I went to visit his grave yesterday?" Adolphus asks from his seat in the hotel conference room next to Deacon Horford Ace.

"Whatever it was, Adolphus," I say, "I'm sure it would be wise to listen to him. He was a great man."

"That he was. That he was."

Adolphus stands and starts pacing the room. I've seen him preach and he puts the fear of God in his parishioners with his 6-foot-4, 300-pound frame and booming, baritone voice. Hell, he put the fear of God in me when he said before the last election that he was going to throw his support behind one of my opponents unless I promised to sign an important civil rights bill that had been sitting on the desk of my predecessor for months.

I promised, got Adolphus' endorsement and won the state of Alabama. I didn't tell Adolphus that I planned to pass Bill 227 anyway.

"My grandfather -- and I loved him more than that sorry ass father of mine who ran out me when I was 12 -- would have sat on the capitol steps until they carted his black ass off to jail," Adolphus says. "My grandfather, God rest his soul, would have told his congregation to pray to the Lord, that the Lord would listen, that their day in the sun was coming if they just followed the good book."

"Amen," Tarik says from his seat on the couch next to me. Tarik is an atheist, but Adolphus has a way of instilling the fear of God in believers and non-believers alike.

"Like I was saying," Adolphus continues, fixing Tarik with a stare that lets my Chief of Staff know that he should never, ever interrupt the Reverend Adolphus Lewis when he is on a roll, "my grandfather would have told his people to pray and be patient and read the good book and a lot of other shit."

Uh, oh.

"But that was then. This is now. Things ain't changed. White folk killed Black folk then. White folk still killing Black folk now. All that non-violence bought us time, Mr. President, but I believe we're running out of it. You know what Biblical passage my grandfather reminded me of at his grave today?"

"What, Adolphus?"

"Leviticus 24, 17: Whoever takes a human life shall surely be put to death. My grandfather is dead, the victim of a White man's bullet, and I don't think he'd be preaching nonviolence today."

"We'll get whoever did this," I say.

"I expect you will. And I expect you will do it quickly. Otherwise, I wouldn't be much of a grandson if I didn't tell my congregation what my grandfather told me from the grave today."

CHAPTER 18

Shirley Harper was a one-term senator from Georgia when I asked her to be my running mate. She could have said no. In fact, most political pundits thought she made a mistake, cutting short a brilliant but short stint as the only Black female senator to spend the next four years kissing babies, cutting ribbons and publicly agreeing with me.

But she said yes, giving me a good chance to pick off a few Southern states and carry the Black vote nationally. She also helped me carry the younger vote – she is 42 but looks 32 – and Shirley Harper now is one heartbeat away from the presidency.

Come to think of it, maybe her decision wasn't so selfless. I had a much-publicized heart attack 10 years ago and Harper, although she always has my back in public, often raises my blood pressure when the cameras are off.

"You should address the public alone, Mr. President," she says after I convene a meeting in the Oval Office and ask her to go on national TV with me to talk about Birmingham.

"No, we should address the nation together. This country is divided, and it's divided along racial lines. We need to be role models. We need to show that this isn't a Black issue. It isn't a White issue. It's a human issue."

"You don't think it will look like you're trotting me out as your African American show pony."

"I hope not, Shirley. Fact is, I don't know."

"Okay. Let's do it. Hey, it might help with my approval numbers."

I take the lead, but only briefly as Shirley and I sit next to each other behind the Oval Office desk that night.

It's an easy introduction. Shirley accomplished so much before she decided to become my running mate and may have accomplished more than any vice president in history during her short stint as VP.

She was the angel on my shoulder, telling me to veto the first gun reform act that came across my desk because it was too weak.

She was the loudest voice in the room – no easy feat with Tarik in the room, too – when we argued back and forth on whether we should increase aid to Israel during a Palestinian – Israeli dustup in my first year as President. Most of the people in that room told me that we already were giving enough. Shirley reminded me that Israel was our strongest ally in the Middle East and "we can't nickel-and-dime them, literally, to death."

Tonight, she is trying to help me defuse a racial bomb.

"I've been to Ezekiel Baptist," Shirley starts. "With my grandmother. With my great-aunt, who makes the best cornbread in the country. Damn, I miss those days. And, Aunt Lilah, if you're listening, can you send some cornbread. These fancy White House chefs can't hold a candle to you."

Shirley pauses. Pulls out a handkerchief and brushes away what looks like a tear. If it was any other politician, I'd think she was acting. Shirley isn't any other politician.

"I could have been in that church Sunday! My nieces, my nephews could have been in that church Sunday!" Adolphus Jones has Shirley by about 200 pounds but I'd rather face his wrath than the anger Shirley is directing at the camera. "This was an attack on me, on Black people all over this country. Hell, it was an attack on this country, period, Blacks and Whites alike. We're better than this, people. We're better than this. But today, two days after yet another senseless killing, I am having a hard time believing it."

I'm not sure I would have put it that way, but Shirley's words really aren't the point. It's her emotion. Black people, I'm sure, already feel it. I want White people to feel it, too, and know of one White person – me – who is feeling it more because I've heard Shirley deliver her speech.

"I have instructed the Department of Justice to look into this," I say. "This wasn't just a mass murder. It was a hate crime and, God knows, there is far too much hate in what I still consider the greatest country in the world. We will be working hand in hand with Alabama authorities. I promise you, we will ferret out the person or persons responsible for one of the darkest days in American history."

Now, I am crying. Hopefully, the cameras don't capture it. A president is supposed to exude strength.

Hell, who cares if they see me shed a tear? And who cares that I don't end our joint speech with my canned ending: "God Bless America."

It ends with Shirley and I hugging before we walk out of the room.

CHAPTER 19

I'm in Dr. Carty's office the next day.

Only two people other than Dr. Carty know I am here: Buddy, the Secret Service agent who waits outside the door, and Ariana, who urged me to see Dr. Carty when I couldn't get to sleep after Shirley and I spoke to the nation.

Buddy thinks I am playing chess with a friend I haven't seen since college. Ariana knows better.

"You skipped your meds again," Ariana said while I was tossing and turning under the presidential covers.

"I'm excited. Shirley and I were good. Damn good."

"I checked your pill vial. You're risking everything."

She's right. With Israel – Palestine, the Birmingham shooting, preparations for the presidential election and all the other "normal" presidential stuff going on, I've forgotten to take my meds a number of times in recent weeks. The last time that happened, it almost ended my relationship with Ariana.

Her name was Shawna. I loved Ariana, had decided to propose and, the night before I popped the question, slept with a woman I met in a bar. I attributed it to my commitment problems but Ariana, after my conscience forced me to tell Ariana about Shawna, attributed it to two symptoms associated with mania: risk-taking and hypersexuality.

Fortunately for me, Ariana stayed.

Fortunately for me, I have Dr. Carty around whenever I might be on the verge of a manic or a depressive episode.

"What did you think of the speech?" I ask Eric.

"Are you asking me as your psychiatrist or as a normal person?"

"Both."

"Is anybody really normal? When you started seeing me, didn't I tell you that normal was in the eyes of the beholder. Was Mozart normal? No. Barry Bonds? No, and I'm not even talking about the performance enhancing drugs he supposedly used to break the home run record. It's important for a person to accept his, if I can coin a term -- 'abnormalcy' -- and work with it to be the best abnormal person he can be. I normally don't tell clients that but, hey, you aren't a normal client. You're President of the United States."

One of the things I like best about Eric is that he isn't the stereotypic psychiatrist you see on TV: reserved, overly earnest, never offering an opinion until the client comes to his own conclusion. Dr. Carty tells me when he thinks I am full of shit. And he has a sense of humor – sometimes I think he'd rather be a standup comedian than a psychiatrist – and I've been seeing him long enough to know that this is standup shtick.

"But, seriously, folks," I say.

"You want me to be serious when you're not taking your mental health seriously?"

"It was that obvious?"

"To me, yes. To the rest of the country, no."

Dr. Carty noticed the same manic tells he saw during my last nationally televised speech: excessive blinking, too much fidgeting, pressured speech.

"You said all the right things. And that Vice-President of yours, she was even better. Watch out for her. You go bat-shit crazy, and they'll invoke the 25th Amendment just to get her into the Oval Office."

Dr. Carty shakes his head, gets up and starts pacing his office.

"I took this job because I really care about you," he says after he sits down.

"Thank you."

"But I'll give it up if you don't start listening to me. You could be – hell, you are – a great president. But you won't be a great president anymore if you don't take your meds. Hell, you won't be a good husband, a good father, a good anything. You're playing with fire. Keep doing it and you won't be the only one who gets burned. This whole country will go down in flames with you."

Am I going to lose the best psychiatrist I ever had?

"Stick with me, Eric. I'll do better."

"You better or I'm back in Philly with a normal client slate. It'll be boring, but I'll make a hell of a lot more money treating accountants, lawyers and a whole bunch of people who aren't President of the United States."

I'm ashamed. I let Eric down. I let Ariana down. I let myself down. Pretty soon, if I don't pay attention to my mental health, I'll let the country down. And a president who lets his country down is a dangerous thing.

"I don't want to go back to Philly," Eric says as I get up to leave. "But I'll do it even though I care about you."

One thing I didn't like about psychiatrists I saw before Eric was that they were too sterile. They trotted out jargon. They said all the right technical things. But they never told me they cared about me.

We hug.

"See you next week," he says.

"Oops. Forgot. I'll be in the Middle East."

"Just take your meds."

"I will."

"And send pictures."

CHAPTER 20

We're meeting in Jerusalem.

Israelis claims it as their capital. Palestinians claim it as their capital. it is the epicenter of Judaism, Islam and Christianity. When I suggested it as the place I'd meet with Farid and Noah as a follow-up to our Camp David talks, though, I didn't get the response I wanted from my Middle East experts.

"Most of the world looks at Tel Aviv as Israel's capital," one of my Middle East advisors, Zais Pedding, told me. "They'll take it as a slap in the face if you meet in Jerusalem."

"Palestinians claim it as their capital, too," Palestinian bureau chief Mahmoud Raf added. "They've been fighting forever on territorial rights in Old Jerusalem, East Jerusalem. Don't be part of the fight. Pick a neutral site."

But, really, is there any neutral site in the Middle East? Is there any spot where I'll be completely safe, that Noah and Farid will be completely safe? I considered calling off the trip at first and staging a second conference at Camp David before Ariana reminded me of one of my favorite scenes in one of my favorite movies, *A Few Good Men*.

"Do you remember when Tom Cruise went to Guantanamo to ask Jack Nicholson a question he easily could have asked over the phone?" Ariana asked. "He didn't care about the answer. He wanted to see how Nicholson would respond. Don't you want to see how Noah and Farid respond on their home turf? Don't you want to see how Israelis and Palestinians respond to you – while you see how they live – on their home turf?"

Note to self: nominate Ariana for Secretary of State when the current Secretary of State can't take it anymore.

"And one more thing," Ariana added. "I want to pray at the Wailing Wall. I want to visit the Dome of the Rock."

"So, this is a vacation thing for you?"

"Pretty much."

It clearly is more important than a vacation to the press, though.

PNT, DVTV and VOX all are hailing the trip as "historic" and "game-changing" and "monumental."

My old buddy at VOX, Brolin Murphy, said he might even vote for me if I bring peace to the Middle East. And then he laughed, saying any peace I obtain in Palestine will do nothing to stop Iran or any of Iran's terrorist proxies.

Our plane touches down at Jerusalem International Airport at 3 a.m. East Coast time. I have no problem sleeping on planes, and am wide awake to face the press, Noah, Farid and a cast of thousands who, no doubt, will be waiting on the tarmac to kick off a historic event that might garner Brolin Murphy's vote.

Instead, I get two Israeli soldiers, who usher Ariana, Tarik and I into a limousine.

"Israeli intelligence received a report of a terrorist plot," one of the soldiers says. "The Prime Minster thinks it is a hoax but, as you Americans say, better to be safe than to be sorry."

Note to self: don't name Ariana Secretary of State. We would have been safer and less sorry at Camp David.

CHAPTER 21

Ariana, Tarik and I are taken to Noah's apartment in the Katamon section of Jerusalem, best known for the Israeli TV show "Srugin" before Noah and his wife decided they wanted to live here. Noah tells me his wife, Sarah, was a fan of the show and was the driving force behind buying the residence. I'm guessing Noah had a say in it – he's Prime Minister, after all – and picked it because it is young, vibrant and sports a coffee shop on every corner.

"Have you ever had Israeli coffee, Mrs. Pappas?" Noah asks as we sit and drink Israeli coffee. "It is a lot stronger, I suppose, than the coffee you served in your cafes in Philadelphia."

Ariana's expression as she sips cafe hafuch tells me that it is strong, too strong for her tastes. Her barely touched cup of coffee tells me that she will be drinking a lot of tea during the trip.

"It certainly is different than any coffee I've ever had!" Ariana says in a too-perky tone she uses when doesn't like something and tries to be nice.

"Thank you," Noah says.

Ariana is back on my Secretary of State short list. She can make foreign diplomats feel good even when her words, in reality, are bad.

Noah, Sarah, Ariana and I are the only people in the room. I told my Secret Service agents to have coffee and babka at one of the dozens of eateries in the neighborhood.

My old Central High classmate really outkicked his coverage with Sarah.

She is beautiful, smart and funny. The beautiful and smart parts are objective. The funny part is subjective, my definition of anybody who laughs at my jokes.

"Your Jackie Mason impersonation is impeccable," says Sarah, an ex-model who served briefly in the IDF. "How does a goy learn to do impressions of the greatest Yiddish comedian who ever lived?"

"Practice. It drives Ariana up the wall so, naturally, I trot Jackie out whenever I can."

Noah tells me that Farid will arrive tomorrow. Noah wanted this to be a day of sightseeing and talking and sampling strong coffee, although Ariana, no doubt, will opt for tea.

That is fine by me. I wanted to come here to learn about Noah's people in general and about their feelings about the Palestinian conflict in particular. And later, when we visit Farid in Gaza City, I want to take the Gazan pulse.

"Just don't get too friendly with suicide bombers while you are over there," Noah says. "Your relationship won't last very long."

And Noah laughs. I guess you have to develop a gallows humor when death and destruction are part of your everyday life, not just the lead story on American TV stations.

Sarah shows us to our quarters. She then takes us on a tour of the house – I hate house tours; I've seen bathrooms before – which includes a visit to her "painting room."

"It is my Zen place," Sarah says.

Some of the paintings, particularly the paintings of the Negev Desert and the Red Sea, are breathtakingly beautiful. Others, like the one of a woman kneeling and crying next to her fallen child, are breathtakingly sad.

"You are a wonderful artist," Ariana says.

"Even more wonderful," Noah says, entering the room, "is the dinner we will have at Zagar. It is the best Israeli restaurant in Jerusalem, perhaps in the entire world. Until then, my friends, the rest of the day is yours. And none of it will be spent discussing politics."

That is fine with me. I want to tour the cafes – Secret Service agents in tow – and Ariana wants to shop the boutiques with Sarah.

The trip, minus the initial terrorist scare, has started better than I expected.

CHAPTER 22

Noah and I are seated by a big picture window overlooking Narkis Street sipping coffees the next morning. The hustle and bustle remind me of the Italian Market in South Philly, where my Mom took me as a kid and where I still go to DiBruno Brothers for their cheeses and meats whenever I'm in Philadelphia.

Sarah and Ariana are off shopping, security contingents in tow, while Noah and I wait for Farid to arrive so we can go about the business of bringing peace, or a semblance of it, to this part of the world.

"You never much liked me back at Central," Noah says.

I almost spit up my coffee. I don't want world peace to fall apart because of something I might have said or done when I was a teenager.

"It's not that I didn't like you...."

"Honesty, Mr. President. If we're not honest with each other now, how can I trust you later when we're sitting around the negotiating table?"

"Fine. I didn't much like you. But you had a good quality or two."

"For instance?"

"Let me get back to you on that."

The thing is, we were different, too different to hang in the same circles. We are similar in some respects now in that we are focused on our countries and, during this conference, both want to smooth over centuries of ill will between Israelis and Palestinians.

Noah still is more serious than me. But I have graduated from the bathroom humor obsession I had in high school to political humor. I'll have to remind myself to hold back on the joke Tarik told me the other day which involved an Israeli, a Palestinian and a Catholic priest walking into a bar. Then, again....

"I wouldn't get my hopes up too much, Mr. President," Noah says. "This war of ours has been going on longer than we've been alive."

"Call me Evan."

"No, I'll stick with Mr. President. I don't want to slip up later when President Fadal is in the room."

From my vantage point across the Atlantic Ocean, things are improving. There haven't been any terrorist attacks on Israel since the Camp David meeting. Noah has taken initial steps to dismantling one of the West Bank settlements, much to the consternation of the conservative faction of the Israeli government.

I hope to build on the progress we made in Camp David, see the religious sites in Jerusalem and visit Gaza, where other presidents have gone but none have accomplished anything of substance.

"Do you trust President Fadal?" I ask.

"As much as any Israeli Prime Minister can trust someone whose party seeks the destruction of Israel. But he can't change things alone. He'll need buy-in from his people and some of those people still view the destruction of Israel as their highest aspiration."

"Empty hands, Noah."

"Empty what?"

"Empty hands. It's Buddhist. Go into every situation with empty hands and you'll be able to accept anything that comes your way."

Noah laughs.

"You're in Jerusalem, center of three of the world's greatest religions – Judaism, Christianity and Islam – and you're talking Buddhism?"

Just then, we see Farid and two other cars pull up outside. Farid gets out of the first limousine. Big beefy men – his security detail, I assume – get out of the second. Three women – his wives? -- get out of the third.

Camp David, Jerusalem style, is ready to begin.

"Just remember, Mr. President, empty hands," Noah smiles.

"Just remember, Mr. Prime Minister, don't slap President Fadal's hand if he offers it in peace."

CHAPTER 23

The negotiations are going better than expected by the time Farid, Noah and I break for lunch the next day. The only negotiation that hasn't gone well, in fact, is the one I had with Ariana when we went to bed last night.

"You won't have to wear a burqa," I said, pulling out my last negotiating tool in an effort to convince her that a conversion to Islam would be in our family's best interest.

"Your other three wives. They might want to wear them."

"There must be a non-burqa sect."

I still feel the elbow Ariana implanted between my third and fourth rib as I sit across from Noah, Farid, and their right-hand men the next day eating shawarma, tabouleh and – in a nod to the American guy – grilled cheese.

Noah got a lot of blowback from the conservative faction of the Knesset when he proposed dismantling a settlement in the West Bank in exchange for the continuation of a ceasefire that has lasted longer than any ceasefire since the Yom Kippur War.

Farid has been sleeping with armed guards outside his quarters since he jailed Islamic Jihad member Abdul Nadal for his part in a suicide bombing that killed 12 Israelis and three Palestinians in Old Jerusalem last year.

Both men are talking peace, though, and I am heartened. Of course, I have been bluffed out of many pots at our White House poker games and am not sure that Noah and Farid aren't bluffing now to garner American support.

I'm not so happy, though, with Noah's under-secretary, Schlomo Glickstein, and Farid's closest advisor, Asad Sur. Glickstein has been pressing Noah to erect more West Bank settlements, my advisors tell me, and Sur is upset that Farid has thwarted many of Islamic Jihad's violent forays into Israel.

But they are here. Glickstein helped Noah ascend to Prime Minster and his conservative views helped Israel at one time. Sur, my intelligence officers tell me, is Farid's childhood friend.

"I listen to him," Farid told me yesterday. "But I do not adhere to his beliefs. He just wants to be heard."

"He just wants your job," I responded.

"He knows what happens to people who want my job. Allow me to worry about him."

The plight of the destitute in Gaza has been the main topic of our conversation today. Israel is responsible for some of it, retaliating three-fold after rockets launched from Gaza obliterated two Tel Aviv synagogues last year. But Farid, with Sur shaking his head at the negotiating table, admits that schools teaching hatred of all Israelis instead of math and science is a problem, too.

"That is not Israel's problem," Noah says.

"It is Israeli's problem if our children grow up thinking Israel is the enemy. I propose a cultural exchange. Israeli teachers in Gaza. Palestinian teachers in Israel. Understanding each other is the first step toward a long-lasting solution. We'll never understand each other until we cross that cultural divide."

"And you can guarantee the safety of Israeli teachers?"

Sur barely conceals a laugh.

"I can only guarantee my actions," Farid says. "I assure you, I will punish anyone who does not follow my edicts."

Noah is unimpressed. Still, from where I am sitting, we are a lot further along than we were before Camp David or even before these meetings began.

Later, I tell Ariana that things went well. She tells me that she is getting used to Israeli coffee and wants her new friend, Sarah, to visit us in D.C. without Noah in tow.

"One more positive," I mention before turning out the lights. "Farid tells me there are many non-burqa, multi-wife sects that are looking for members."

I assume I will be feeling the effects of Ariana's elbow at the negotiating table again tomorrow.

CHAPTER 24

It's the next-to-last-day of the Jerusalem summit and I am riding a high. Noah and Farid are making headway on a teacher exchange, Gazan teachers teaching Israeli students about life in Gaza and Israeli teachers teaching Gazan children about life in Israel. The program will be administered by the Israeli Teaching Association, over Sur's objections.

Noah, despite Schlomo's objections, has decided to use Israeli funds to construct a Gazan settlement on the West Bank next to a recently constructed Israeli settlement. The neighboring settlements will share water, food and a city council composed of five Israelis and five Palestinians.

"Have you forgotten, Mr. Prime Minster, how many Israelis have died at the hand of terrorists over the last decade?" Schlomo pounded the negotiating table.

"Which is why the neighboring settlements are so important. Israelis and Palestinians working together. Imagine that? And if I can imagine that, maybe Israelis and Palestinians can imagine the same thing and stop viewing each other as enemies."

"But, boss...."

"That last word – boss – I am fond of. It means you serve at my pleasure. And, if you continue to buck me at every turn, it means you will be selling kabobs on the other side of town like you were doing when you were a child."

Farid has invited Noah to tour Palestinian munitions plants and monitor them through an intelligence exchange between the nations. Sur started to object but stopped himself. Maybe, like Glickstein, he was a kabob salesman before his childhood friend elevated him to a more prestigious and, no doubt, higher paying position.

Farid also promised to eliminate the portion in Intifada's charter calling for the extinction of Israel.

"You will be going against all that we, all of Islam, stand for," Sur said.

"Our religion does not stand for the elimination of Israel. And Islamic Jihad, unless we want to continue to wage war with a country that is far superior to us militarily, should not stand for it either."

During a break in the proceedings, I saw Glickstein and Sur talking in the corner, no doubt agreeing that their respective bosses are idiots. I was pleased to see that Tarik wasn't involved in the "my boss is an idiot" conversation.

Ariana and Sarah are enjoying their time together. Ariana and one of Farid's wives – Shanda, I believe, but it's hard to tell with the burka– also have become friends. Ariana now likes the stronger Israeli coffee and might suggest it to the group who bought her coffee company before we moved to Washington.

The press is getting what it wants, good news, something that has been lacking on the Israeli – Palestinian front in a long, long time.

Brolin Murphy led one of his VOX shows with this: "Mr. President, you are doing an outstanding job. It would be my honor and privilege to have you on my show."

Was that Murphy or a body-double?

And Philadelphia native Jack Tanner led his show on PNT with this: "Leave it to a Philly boy to broker peace in the Middle East. The City of Brotherly Love is the city that spawned international love."

And DVTV's Bekka Mornay started her show with this: "Imagine, if you will, that you are in the second grade. And your second-grade teacher gave you a homework assignment, although she didn't explain what the homework assignment was about or even when it was due. Now, imagine that this homework assignment had to be typed, double-spaced…" At some point, I assume, Bekka got around to tying this double-spaced second-grade homework assignment to our Jerusalem talks. But I turned the channel before she got that far.

"Honey, you are married to the man who will go down in history as the person most responsible for bringing peace to the world," I tell Ariana as we snuggle under the covers that night. "A man who will be credited with conquering a previously unconquerable problem, who postponed the fulfillment of the Apocalypse, who...."

"Hasn't taken his meds."

"It's that obvious?"

"Your hyperbole is even more hyperbolic than normal."

"You know what else is even more hyperbolic than normal?" I smile.

"Take your meds first and I'll consider it when you get back to bed."

And I thought Farid and Noah were tough negotiators.

CHAPTER 25

D amn, I was good."

"Don't you mean the conference was good?"

Ariana and I are back at the White House a few days later and I can't sleep. I'm pacing and pacing and pacing and Ariana is waiting patiently in bed. Does she really want to cuddle? I want to oblige but can't get Jerusalem out of my mind.

Peace in the Israel – Palestine conflict.

And next: peace in the entire Middle East!

Peace, brought to you by President Evan Pappas and other bit players at the conference.

"Come to bed," Ariana says.

Damn, this woman is horny. Come to think of it, my sex overdrive is in, well, overdrive and I'm ready to dive under the White House bedroom covers.

"But take your meds first."

"What? I'm amped, so it necessarily means I didn't take my meds?"

"Did you?"

"Uh, no."

I take my meds. It's the first time I've taken them since we've been back in the States, but what's a president to do with all of the media outlets applauding him and with my poll numbers skyrocketing.

Maybe I should see Dr. Carty. No, definitely I should see Dr. Carty. But this high feels great, he'll warn me about mania and that I should return to Planet Earth.

What's so great about being on Planet Earth, anyway? I kind of like the stratosphere I occupy now, flying above the planet, looking down on a peaceful Middle East and a United States populace that, no doubt, will give me a landslide win. Plus, a wife who can't get enough of me.

"Ready?" I say after I vault into bed.

"For sex, no. For a talk, yes."

I hate preliminaries.

"You know, my girlfriends warned me about marrying you," she says. "He's too into himself, he loves the idea of love but not love itself and – the biggie – he's bipolar. Do you really want to be with someone who thinks he can touch God when he can barely touch is toes, they said."

But Ariana said yes, leaving a string of broken hearts behind. I don't know why she chose me – actually, I do know; I'm quite charming – but am glad she did.

It's the best thing that ever happened to me along with adopting Lin. Our talks in the morning, our shared values, and even our unshared values because we can talk about them without arguing. Ariana gets me, maybe the only person other than Tarik, Dr. Carty and my younger sister, Tina, who died five years ago from an unexpected heart attack.

Ariana has seen me through the good: getting elected mayor, then governor and – a shocker to even me – to president. And she's seen me through the bad, a few manic episodes along the way that always resulted from not taking my meds.

Ariana turns out the lights. I turn them back on.

"I thought we were going to...."

"No, we weren't," Ariana says. "You're bordering on manic and probably could have sex twice a day. I can't."

"Can we at least cuddle?"

"I guess. After all, you are the person who single-handedly is bringing peace to the Middle East, who will end racism before you leave the presidency, who can leap tall buildings in a single bound."

"I'd leave the tall buildings part out."

Ariana shakes her head.

"I was kidding. Keep taking your meds or all of those buildings will come crashing down."

CHAPTER 26

Aida Curtain is good at her job. No, she is *great* at her job. I've had, give or take, a dozen press secretaries in my political career and Aida is better than any of them.

My detractors complain that the media is too nice to me, too fawning. And, except for Brolin Murphy, they have a point. But I'm only part of the equation. The other part of the equation is Aida, who charms them every morning even when many of those mornings would turn contentious without Aida's deft touch.

"You should have been a psychologist," I tell her as we wait for others to arrive for our first staff meeting since the Jerusalem trip.

"I have a master's in counseling psychology with a focus on aberrant psychology."

"Aberrant psychology?"

"Perfect when I'm dealing with some of those loonies out there."

She points in the direction of the press room, where she expects to meet today with people from ABC, NBC, PNT, VOX, pretty much all of the outlets hungry for info about the Jerusalem summit.

"Brolin Murphy's the worst," I say.

Curtain smiles.

"Actually, I think he has a thing for me. Have you noticed how nice he's been to you lately?"

And I thought it was peace in the Middle East, a drop in crime, a rise in the economy and all of the other things that have happened recently to boost my approval ratings higher than any president since Bill Clinton.

Silly me.

Tarik straggles in, looking like he's had a long night because, it turns out, he's had a long night.

"The things I do for you," he says.

"For instance?"

"Wining and dining a staff member of Congressman Hamer who, by the way, wants your head served up on a silver platter."

"Would this staff member be female?"

"Yes."

"And was the dinner successful?"

"Define successful."

Jim Banoff is next. I have another gun control town hall next week and want him to prepare preliminary remarks.

My VP, Shirley Harper, joins us. She has enough on her political plate and usually doesn't come to my staff meetings. But Shirley and I need to follow up on the Birmingham shooting with an American public howling for change.

Tarik and Banoff brief me.

Shirley tells me of the meeting she had with the Georgia Civil Rights Commission while I was away.

We finish and Aida practically charges for the door, eager to regale the press with tales of peace in the Middle East.

"Uh, Aida," I say.

She turns, smiling.

"I'm meeting the press today."

Aida no longer is smiling.

"We have an election coming up and I want them to put a face – my face – on all of the good news. But stand by my side and smack me on the head if I screw up."

I'm lucky she doesn't smack me now.

CHAPTER 27

I don't know how Aida does it.

It's way too bright in this press room, so bright that I can barely make out the faces of reporters and photographers in front of me. And it's way too cramped. I stand on the dais in front of Congress to deliver my State of the Union message and there's a distance between me and the audience, not to mention a teleprompter I use except when I go off the cuff to deliver something I invariably find witty, and Ariana invariably chastises me for later.

Tarik is off to the side along with Aida and a few other staff members. He is smiling, but I don't know if it's a nervous smile because he thinks I'll bomb this press conference or a confident smile because he knows I'll give the reporters – and the nation – a performance they'll never forget. Aida looks nervous, though, and I don't know why. She's watched me kill in front of larger groups – I still can't believe they let me throw out the first ball in that Phillies games – and has been with me when I met with more hostile audiences. Hey, it could have been very hostile last week, me sitting with leaders of always-warring Palestine and Israel. But that worked out fine, almost as fine as that first pitch I threw at the Phillies game, a strike down the middle with juice. I'm surprised they didn't try to sign me to a contract on the spot.

"I know you guys are used to Aida, so let me apologize up front," I start. "But she's nearby, in case I screw up. Please don't make me screw up, guys."

I won't, but a little self-deprecating humor goes a long way.

Jim DelRusso from PNT has the first question. I've seen enough of these conferences to know that he always goes first and always lobs softballs

Aida's way. Start with a bang, go out with a bang and everybody will forget what happens in between. I know that from giving speeches and Aida – she'll be a great psychologist if she ever gets tired of this press secretary thing – knows it, too.

"Kudos, Mr. President," Jim starts.

"Thanks, Jim."

"I've been doing this for a long time – my wife tells me too long – and I thought I'd never see the day when we had peace in the Middle East."

"Is there a question in there somewhere?"

"No, I just wanted to say thank you."

That was easy. Maybe I give Aida too much credit. My daughter could have handled that. Hell, Jim Banoff could have handled that, and he has the worst stage fright I've ever seen. There's a reason he got into the speech writing business. He has the words. He just can't deliver them.

Diana DuBois from DVTV is next. I've seen Diana ambush a President or two – all Republican – and there's a chance she'll ambush me. Actually, I hope she tries to ambush me. It'll give me a chance to show how nimble I am on my oratory feet.

"As Jim said, Mr. President, kudos for what you did in Jerusalem," Diana starts. "But that was just a one-week summit. How, exactly, do you plan to achieve peace in the Middle East when no president before you has been able to do it."

"I don't have a tough act to follow, then."

A couple of laughs, but not as many as the line deserved. A tough crowd, these reporters.

"But seriously, folks, it won't be easy. It's why presidents before me have failed when their intentions were just as good as mine. But it's a different day now. A different time. I have known Prime Minister Abrams for decades. Our relationship alone will provide motivation for him to stop the killing. But it's much more than that. He has seen too many of his people die and – you'd only know this if you sat across the table from him like I did last week – he is sick of it. And President Fadal, unlike other Palestinian leaders before him, is a true visionary. He looks forward, not backward to all of the slights and perceived slights his people have experienced. With Noah and Farid – drink araq with a couple of guys long into the night and you're on a first-name basis – working with me, I am confident that we have blazed a new path."

Did I ramble? It seems like I was rambling? And if I was rambling, did I make any sense? Tarik still is smiling, but Aida is shaking her head. Maybe I should have let her handle this one. Nah, I'm doing great. And this is only a half-hour press conference. My rambling – if it qualifies as rambling – ate up time and we only have a few minutes left.

Time enough for New York Beacon reporter Doug Peterman. The New York Beacon used to be known as the Grand Old Lady of newspapers. All the news that's fit to print and all that crap. I read it when I was in college, although I always thought their sports page was too skimpy. Doug is the grand old reporter – old, anyway – and he won't be as easy on me as DelRusso or DuBois.

Bring it on, Doug. Did I say that out loud? These lights are going in and out of focus. Did I take my meds last night? I'm sure I did. Actually, I'm not sure, but it doesn't matter. I handled Noah and Farid. What's a little, old – the emphasis on "old" – New York Beacon reporter going to do to me?

"Your critics say you are overreaching," Peterman starts. "What's more, they say that your meeting with Prime Minster Abrams and President Fadal has nothing to do with bringing peace to the Middle East. They say it has everything to do with the election in November. If there's peace, you win a second term. If, as has happened before, the peace process breaks down, you can spin things to make it look like you made progress. My question...."

"Good. I had a feeling there was a question in there somewhere."

What's with these lights?

"My question..."

"And I'm sure it will be a good one. People say the New York Beacon is failing, but I'm not one of those people. And, if it is failing, it isn't failing because of you, Dougie boy."

The room? It's starting to get smaller. But what do they say about rooms? There are no small rooms, only small ruminators. Or something like that.

"Flattery will get you nowhere, Mr. President."

Damn.

"My question: can you lay out the process which will help you monitor the situation in Israel and Palestine? In the entire Middle East, if it comes to that? The process you'll use whereby you'll maintain the safety of the Israeli teachers going into a land which, heretofore, has vowed to exterminate Israel."

Whereby? Heretofore? Peterman certainly knows fancy words, although I'm guessing most of the country, and maybe even some of his New York Beacon readers, wouldn't know what he is talking about.

"I've talked about this at length before in impromptu meetings with the press," I say. "Weren't you there, Doug? Were you out golfing?"

Tarik isn't smiling anymore. Aida looks terrified.

"Is golf really a sport, Doug? I mean, you hit a little white ball, you get in a cart, and you drive to where that little white ball landed, probably far away from where you intended, Dougie. Then you hit it again and – I'm guessing in your case, Douglas – hit it about 10 more times before you put it in the hole...."

Is that a buzz I hear? Is it from the crowd? Inside my head?

"So, getting back to my initial question – is golf a real sport? – I say no. It's mostly driving around in a cart with a few breaks in between. Anyway, go to hell, Doogie."

Why is Tarik rushing to the podium? Why is Aida grabbing my elbow and telling me to "limp offstage" before she takes her customary role behind the dais?

Later, Aida says she told reporters that I had gout and was having a bad reaction to a steroid, prednisone.

Not a truthful answer, but a good one. A country can deal with a president who has the gout. A country probably can't deal with a president who has bipolar and goes manic when he doesn't take his meds.

CHAPTER 28

What was I doing?

What the hell was I doing?

It's not like I haven't gone manic before when I didn't take my meds. There was the time after law school when Tarik, me and a couple of buddies celebrated graduation with a trip to Vegas. I celebrated a little too much, wound up swimming naked in Caesar Palace's pool and nobody – except Tarik, who still teases me about it to this day – knew about my illness.

There was the time a year after I was elected mayor of Philadelphia when I was involved in a contentious battle over parking meters – *parking meters! --* and didn't sleep three straight nights. I chalked my lack of sleep up to parking meters but Dr. Carty, who I had been seeing for about a decade at the time, pointed out that I hadn't been taking my meds during my parking meter preoccupation.

And there was the time after I was elected governor of Pennsylvania by the widest margin in state history. I went skiing in the Poconos. One problem, though. I didn't know how to ski and broke my leg. Dr. Carty again pointed out that I hadn't taken my meds and we started talking about my penchant for self-sabotaging when things were going too well.

Is that what I was doing when I gave the press conference from hell? Things had been going well, maybe too well for my psychological liking.

Shit!

"Will you snap out of it already? This is getting pretty boring."

Thank God, I have Ariana. She has spent all of her time with me over the last week, listening to my ranting, watching me beat myself up, forcing me to eat. My White House chef, James Asher, has done his part by making lobster dishes three straight nights and Tarik did his part by driving to Philly to pick up a dozen Pat's cheesesteaks. My self-loathing only increased, though, after I finished my third steak with fried onions and realized that I put on a couple of pounds.

"Quit," Ariana says.

"Huh?"

"Quit the presidency. Your Vice President is perfectly capable of doing your job. It's about time we had a female president, anyway."

I think Ariana is kidding about me quitting, although she's right about Shirley. She'd do a great job, either when I'm voted out of office in November or, assuming I can weather this self-imposed storm, I win and serve out a second term.

While Ariana has tended to me, my staff has tended to the business of running the country. Aida telling me to limp offstage was improvised brilliance. Her uncle takes prednisone for gout and had a prednisone-induced manic episode. She knows I have gout – it's my canned excuse whenever Tarik beats me in a game of one-on-one – and figured I could blame the prednisone.

Shirley has done a wonderful job dealing with the press. She wasn't with me in Jerusalem, but you wouldn't know it the way she talks about the nuts and bolts of the talks and how we will proceed going forward. She also stepped in for me at a town hall about race relations the other night. According to Doug Peterman at the Beacon, "the Vice President looked very presidential." Peterman might have an axe to grind after I used him as a punching back at the press conference, but he is right. Hopefully, Shirley will put her presidential aspirations on the shelf until I'm ready to step down.

"Are you ready to step down?" I know I'm not talking out loud. I've been back on my meds since the press conference and am almost at 100 percent. This is just Ariana reading my mind. It happens when you've been married so long.

"No, but I'm ready to step out of this room. I'm going to call Tarik. I feel like hooping."

CHAPTER 29

I want to go on national television and tell the nation that I suffer from bipolar disorder, that the man they witnessed speaking irrationally at a press conference was an example of someone who didn't take his bipolar meds, that I have dealt with mental illness for 30 years and have been a good husband, a good father and a good public servant all along.

That's what I want to do. But I can't. This country has come a long way in its treatment and acceptance of mental illness. Whether they accept a president with bipolar or not, as Tarik reminds me during our pickup game, is a different matter.

"Thomas Eagleton," he says when I ask him whether I should tell the truth. "Thomas Eagleton."

Eagleton was a U.S. senator from Missouri from 1968 to 1987. He suffered from depression, something his handlers kept secret from the public until it became very, very public after George McGovern tabbed him as his Vice-Presidential running mate in 1972. Word leaked and McGovern dropped Eagleton. The fact that Eagleton continued to serve as a Missouri senator through 1987 tells me that Missouri voters thought he governed well enough despite the depression.

"Serving as senator is one thing," Tarik says before he hits a foul-line jumper. "Serving as vice president one heartbeat away from the presidency is another thing. But serving as president – which you are, for the time being – is quite another."

We don't talk about the 25th Amendment, which allows for the removal of a president if he can't perform his duties. I'm sure Trey Collins, the frontrunner for the Republican nomination and Griffin Johnston, who is leading in the Democratic primaries, have their aides parsing the amendment comma by comma this morning.

I drive to the basket to tie the game. Tarik elbows me on his way to the hoop to take a one-point lead and I hit three straight jumpers to win the game and remind my old friend that I'm the boss on the court which, in our minds, is almost as important as being the boss of the country.

"Not bad for a guy with gout."

"You know it's not gout."

"I also know Thomas Eagleton never got a chance to play on a basketball court at the White House."

Tarik is right politically, but is he right when it comes to the greater good? Wouldn't it be better if we could accept that people can function well with mental illnesses, that they can even become one of the greatest presidents ever – is that my mania speaking? -- with a mental illness.

Dr. Carty, who I haven't seen since my meltdown, will agree with me at our appointment later. Hell, I always want people to agree with me. Just because I'm President doesn't mean that I left that universal affliction – the need to be right – at the White House door.

Eric has spent his entire life treating people with mental illnesses and I'm sure a number of them, including me, owe their lives to him. If I came clean to the American public with Dr. Carty's approval, if I can serve as a role model for Americans with mental illness, Eric will help more people than he has helped in his entire career.

Then, again...

"You have an election coming up," Eric says after we discuss the press conference, the gout excuse, self-sabotage and whether I can bring a Pat's steak to him at my next visit. "You lose and you won't be a role model for anyone. You win – and your odds of winning are better if the voters think you're sane – and you can say whatever you want."

Et tu, Eric?

I settle down in front of the TV that night, tell Ariana what Eric said, and she smiles.

"Good. It'll give me more time to redecorate this place, plant a few more roses in the Rose Garden and do a couple of other things: like promoting women's rights, something you've woefully ignored."

"Seriously?"

"You'll seriously be looking for another job if you tell people that you have bipolar. Let it rest for now."

We watch a couple of "Seinfeld" reruns and one "Curb Your Enthusiasm" before going to bed. I swear, Seinfeld and Curb are more therapeutic than any med I take.

"By the way," Ariana says before she turns out the lights. "Lin's coming home tomorrow."

Seeing Lin is therapy for me. I'll be 100 percent in no time.

CHAPTER 30

Lin has been away at Northwestern since September, and I miss her. Maybe if she was around, I wouldn't be screwing up so badly. I get all wrapped up in world affairs and domestic affairs and presidential campaigns and I forget the most important thing in my life: my daughter.

It's called perspective, and I've been sorely lacking in it lately.

Perspective arrives at 9 a.m. the next morning. Ariana is off doing some important First Lady business, I'm deep into the boring nuts and bolts of an infrastructure bill I should have dispensed with months ago and am fretting about a 25th Amendment challenge I could face if the cabinet doesn't buy my gout excuse.

"Hello!"

I might be crazy, but I still can run the country. Republicans and Democrats just want me out of the picture so they can go about the business of nominating a couple of mediocre candidates without an incumbent president to worry about. Twenty-fifth Amendment, my ass.

"Is anybody home?"

And then there's gun control and deteriorating race relations and a few hiccups in the Israel – Palestine negotiations. I never really liked alcohol, but this seems like as good a time as any to start drinking.

"Mr. President, can I please have an audience?"

I look up. It's Lin, my favorite audience. We hug -- tighter than normal -- and she throws her suitcase on the Oval Office couch.

"Where do you go when you're daydreaming?" Lin asks.

"Jerusalem. Birmingham. The usual places."

"Well, come home for now. There's something I need to talk about."

My press conference meltdown? Lin certainly isn't shielded from the news at Northwestern. She's talked with Ariana a few times since, but I was too ashamed – and too tied up with myself – to talk to her.

"Yeah, I know. I need to take my meds. It won't happen again."

"This is about me. You're President and you think everything is about you?"

Lin tells me about a course she thinks she is failing. I've heard this refrain, and it never comes true. She is carrying a 3.9 GPA.

But her confidence is lacking. Is it because her biological mother left her in a vegetable garden in Guang Zhou because of China's one-child policy? Is it because she's the president's daughter and isn't treated like other students? Is it a boy? I swear, I'll kill him.

"I had another panic attack," Lin says.

Lin has had anxiety issues for much of her life. She was misdiagnosed at first – ADHD, the first quack psychiatrist said – before we figured out what it was. She tried a few meds, most with bad side effects, until she hit on Wellbutrin.

Since then, it's been smooth sailing. Until now.

"I'm sitting in class one day, nothing special, and I started feeling nervous, really nervous," she says. "I had trouble breathing. My heart was racing. I finally had to leave class before anybody else noticed, although my friend, Janie, said she could tell even though she was sitting 10 rows away."

"Oh, honey." My heart breaks for her. She's such a good girl and still goes through this.

What's a parent to do? But, as Lin said, this isn't about me. Sometimes, the best thing to do is listen.

"Anyway, I came back to class the next day – Psychology 101, ironically – and my teacher pulled me aside after class and asked what was wrong."

"What did you tell him?"

"Her. I made up some excuse, that I was up studying for finals three straight nights and hadn't slept."

"Did she buy it."

"Yep. But I didn't like that I said it. The teacher's a psychologist. I couldn't even tell a psychologist, who would know about these things, who would empathize with these things? Anyway, I told her the next day."

"And?"

"And everything's okay. No panic attacks since. I even got an A in the class."

"Good."

"For me, maybe. How about for you?"

What is she talking about? And then it strikes me. Lin is talking about herself, but the message is directed at me. Lin came clean, feels better about herself and even aced finals.

Me? I haven't come clean, don't feel better about myself, and don't know if I'll ace my ultimate test: the election.

"It's not so simple, honey."

"Why not?"

"How about if we have lunch?"

"It's too early."

"Breakfast?"

"Too late. We'll talk about it later and I'll really tell you how lame I think your gout excuse is and how much good you could do for the mentally ill if you admitted you were bipolar."

CHAPTER 31

Trey Collins still is prattling on about "The President's Meltdown" two weeks later.

"If this isn't cause to invoke the 25th Amendment, I don't know what is," he says during an hour-long sit-down with Sean McGill. "And he expects us to believe he had gout? My great, great grandfather had gout and all it did was stop him from eating shellfish, not going ballistic in a press conference."

McGill laughed. Even Ariana laughed as we watched.

"You're supposed to be on my side," I said.

"Collins suggesting that gout would stop you from eating lobster? That's funny. He doesn't know about your love affair with crustaceans."

I don't know if Collins wants me to bow out or if he thinks it will be easier beating me in the next election if he can label me "The Crazy President" -- the title various VOX hosts have been using – when I run.

Collins slipped up during the McGill interview, though. He talked about me wearing a fake nose and glasses at the next State of the Union. I deliver another State of the Union in February and that will mean I won the election in November. Collins must think he can't beat me without smearing me. He is just practicing good politics although I remember it being called "dirty politics" a long, long time ago.

Today, though, I won't be talking about anything as sexy as elections or crazy presidents or even nuclear warfare, which always seems to get a rise out of my staff.

I'll be talking infrastructure at my staff meeting, but not about anything substantive in a bill I still haven't signed because it falls woefully short of giving the American people what they need to fix their roads, build their bridges and do a whole bunch of other things that affect them in their daily lives.

I'll be talking about the word itself: "infrastructure." Is there a word in the English vocabulary – I don't consider "John Kasich" a word – more boring than infrastructure? I want my staff to help me come up with a word I can use in speeches, in interviews and when I finally hit the campaign trail. Let my opponents keep saying infrastructure while putting voters to sleep. I'll call it something else and the voters, I tell myself, will be energized and eager to vote for a me even if they think I'm crazy.

"How about 'Sex-frastructure,'" Tarik offers.

The staff laughs, the only laughs I have ever heard in a staff meeting about infrastructure. I've noticed that Tarik has been talking a lot about sex recently. I know a smart, attractive and age-appropriate woman who likes him and make a mental note to set up a double-date.

"Pothole Potpourri," Banoff says.

"I like alliteration," I say. "And everybody can identify with big-time mechanic bills after their cars get swallowed up in potholes. But it doesn't go far enough."

"Fixing Stuff." It's Aida Curtain. Aida probably is the most articulate person in the room. She also has her finger on the pulse of the people, although I think she wanted her hands wrapped around my throat when I sent her out the other day practically emptyhanded to deal with a press still howling about my press conference misstep.

"Close," I say.

Aida smiles and takes a bow.

"But not close enough. Let's keep working on it. I'll work on twisting arms in Congress."

Everybody files out except Tarik?

"Sex-frastructure?" I say.

"Hey, I got everybody's attention."

"Are you getting anything else?"

Tarik doesn't respond. He can talk nuclear war, presidential elections and economics, but he shuts down whenever I bring up his personal life.

"Maybe if I didn't have to work 20-hour days keeping a crazy president in office."

"I can fix that. You're off Saturday, except for dinner with Ariana, me and a woman I know who has terrible taste in men."

CHAPTER 32

Part I of the Israel – Palestine cultural exchange went well. The works of Palestinian poets and artists Mahmoud Darwish, Suheir Hammad and Farah Chamma didn't draw many to the Jerusalem Museum of Modern Art in the beginning, if you exclude the protesters who picketed outside the museum. As the weeks went by, though, more and more Israelis came to know the beauty of Palestinian art.

The works of Israeli artists got a more tepid greeting at the Gaza Cultural Center at the outset owing, in part, to a threat from Islamic Jihad opposition that anyone attending the exhibits would be met with strong reprisals. But Farid jailed Islamic Jihad Cultural Minister Baba Il-Hassein and promised Gazans that there would be no reprisals. Many Gazans viewed the works of Yael Eisenberg, Haim Gouri and Karen Pelese. One even wrote a laudatory review in the Gaza Times. The author used a pseudonym for safety purposes, but the fact that it was published at all in a newspaper that had been virulently anti-Israel is progress.

"You have me to thank for this," I tell Ariana as we're reading New York Beacon accounts over breakfast one day. "I'm the one who is solely responsible for bringing peace in the Middle East, for accomplishing what most – including you, honey – thought couldn't be accomplished, for pretty much everything that is good in this world."

"Did you stop taking your meds?"

"I'm teasing. That won't happen again."

Part II of what we plan to call The Middle East Accords, the teacher exchange, has been more problematic. It was difficult enough rounding up enough Israeli and Gazan teachers to cross the border. It was even tougher ensuring their safety and, after a bomb exploded near a Gazan school on the first day of the teacher exchange, I thought we might have to scuttle the idea.

"Let me deal with the bomber," Abrams said.

And he did. Abrams learned that a member of the archly conservative wing of the Knesset knew of terrorist plans to detonate the bomb. But he kept the information to himself. The Knesset member has been censured and Noah has strongly encouraged him to resign before he is drummed out of the government.

Still, Abrams and Farid have decided to put the teacher exchange on hold.

The American press have been hailing Parts I and II as "an unmitigated success," "the groundwork for a lasting peace" and "President Pappas' finest hour." But I'm more interested in what the Israeli and Palestinian press have to say. For the most part, they haven't been as effusive as PNT, DVTV or even my old buddy, Brolin Murphy at VOX, but the headline in the Jerusalem Times two days ago, "Peace with Palestine?" had me breaking open a champagne bottle at one of my staff meetings later that day.

"Remember, Mr. President, this is the easy part," Middle East advisor Herm Romol said. "There's Nakbar. There's Iran. And you've only made steps – baby steps, in my opinion – with Israel and Palestine."

"Enough with the negative waves," I say, quoting Oddball from one of my favorite World War II movies, *Kelly's Heroes*. "Enjoy the champagne."

Later, Tarik reminds me that most of my staff members hadn't been born when *Kelly's Heroes* came out in 1970.

He also keeps asking me for the name of the woman I am setting him up with for our White House double date tonight. But I want it to be a surprise and don't want Tarik using his Defcom computer clearance to unearth every detail about his date beforehand.

"Just be yourself," I say.

"That's all you got?"

"Or don't be yourself. It hasn't been working."

CHAPTER 33

Tarik should have married Aidalle. She was smart, she was beautiful and she laughed at his jokes. But she also beat him in the Temple Law School moot court competition.

"It's not that I have a fragile male ego," Tarik told me after ending the best romantic relationship of his life. "But I don't want to spend all my time arguing over who picks up the check with a woman who argues better than I do."

"You'd save money," I said.

He also should have married Janine. She was an artist, someone Tarik met in Rittenhouse Square where she was displaying artwork that should have been hanging in a museum.

She made Tarik look at things differently, had more of an artistic bent than anyone I have ever known and was pretty in a cute, not glamorous, way.

"She isn't into politics," Tarik told me after he broke up with Janine.

"So?"

"What are we supposed to talk about?"

The good thing about Tarik from a Chief of Staff standpoint is that he can make any situation look good. No doubt in my mind, I wouldn't have been elected mayor and then governor and then president without my lifelong friend making voters think I'm better than I am.

The bad thing about Tarik from a relationship standpoint is that he can make any woman look bad. Tarik will notice the tiny blemish at first, turn that blemish into all he notices after a while and use it to ruin relationships in the end.

"Why are you so afraid of commitment?" I asked Tarik a while back after he broke up with a Victoria's Secret model who was in her third year of med school.

"I'm not afraid of commitment. I'm afraid of committing to the wrong one."

I know a little something about fearing commitment. I spent more than half of my life until I met Ariana avoiding it. I'm not sure where it came from, although a clinical psychologist I broke up with told me it was tied to my father's death. When I knew as I got older that I needed someone, I battled through my commitment problems.

Tarik's fear – and I'm channeling Dr. Carty here – comes from a tumultuous upbringing. He was brought up in a two-parent household, but it was one of the most dysfunctional two-parent households I ever saw. His father beat his mother with a lug wrench one night when he thought she was cheating. Poor, little Tarik saw it and, I'm sure, carries that image with him whenever he starts to come close to someone.

"Just give this one a chance," I tell Tarik as Ariana and Tarik's blind date, Israeli diplomat Rachel Malki, prepare dinner in the White House kitchen.

"You don't think me going out with an Israeli diplomat will look like a conflict of interest with everything we have going on in the Middle East?"

"Is that the excuse you plan to use when you inevitably break up with her two-and-a-half months down the road?"

"Two-and-a-half-months?"

"I've been with you a long time. I set my calendar by it."

Ariana and Rachel come out with a meal that would cement U.S. - Israeli relations for decades to come if, in fact, there was a problem with U.S. -

Israeli relations. Ariana made her special-occasions lobster salad, a dish that would have won my heart if Ariana already hadn't won it by our third date. I asked her to let Rachel steal the show, but Ariana didn't listen to me and made a chocolate lava cake that would have made chocolate lava cakes in Paris convert to strawberry short cakes.

Rachel brings out shakshouka, something she calls me'orav yerulshami and lamb kabobs. She also made something called sufganiyot for desert, although I'm betting on Ariana's chocolate lava cake to, ahem, take the cake.

"A woman who is beautiful, smart and can cook, Tarik," I announce when we start eating.

Tarik responds with a kick under the table.

Rachel, it turns out, was a member of the Israeli army before Noah felt she would serve him better on the diplomatic side. Her two grandparents died at Auschwitz. Her parents are Orthodox Jews and Rachel says she is "Jewish by culture. The religion part, I'm not so sure."

Ariana and I spend the rest of the dinner trying to facilitate the conversation – *"Tarik and I used to do Jewish deli whenever we were in Philly"; "Rachel loves sports too, Tarik"; "Tarik's the one who pushed the Jerusalem summit, not me"* – but we didn't need to.

"As much as I love you guys," Tarik says, "will you get the hell out of here?"

I look back at a smiling Tarik and Rachel, their hands touching on top of the table, as Ariana and I move to another room.

I've seen this look with Tarik before. I've also seen this look turn to fear, which inevitably turns into ruined relationships.

"Do you think they have a chance?" Ariana says as we walk by a portrait of FDR.

"They better. Peace in the Middle East depends on it."

CHAPTER 34

We're only two primaries in, and it's looking like one of the most boring presidential election seasons ever.

The Republicans have held three debates, winnowing the number of candidates from 10 to seven to four, but there really is only one candidate who matters and who, no doubt, will be the Republican nominee come convention time: Trey Collins.

Collins has a number of things going for him. He is charismatic. He is good looking. And – a prerequisite in presidential politics these days – he is ruthless. His main challenger before the Iowa caucuses was Diane Dort, but leaked photos before Iowa showed Dort with a man not her husband sneaking in and out of hotel lobbies. Dort said she was appalled – *"When did this party sink so low?"* -- and said the man was one of her husband's ex-classmates.

The man, it turned out, *was* one of her husband's ex-classmates. Republican frontrunner and probable leaker Trey Collins said that made things worse even after the New York Beacon and Washington Guardian later came out with stories saying that Dort and her husband's friend were booking a surprise birthday party for her husband at the hotel.

"We are the family values party," Collins intoned in a speech before Iowa. "With all due respect, the values Senator Dort appears to hold dear – not the only thing she holds dear, apparently -- are not the values we want to impart on our children."

Dort dropped out after finishing seventh in Iowa.

Things haven't been as salacious on the Democratic side, although a few Democratic senators have told me in confidence that they wished things were spicier. Griffin Johnston, 79-year-old Griffin Johnston, has stood for the same things since the Peloponnesian War. Voters, pundits and pretty much everybody refer to him as "Uncle Griffin." Good, old Uncle Griffin. Even his wife has been caught off-mike a few times calling him "Uncle Griffin." VOX speculated for weeks after the remarks on Jane and Griffin's true relationship.

Uncle Griffin took the New Hampshire primary, beating a couple of non-entities after a record-low turnout. He also won Iowa and is expected to take South Carolina.

VOX looked deeper into the New Hampshire results, though, to find a number that made Senator Johnston look vulnerable.

"Yes, good, old Uncle Griffin, won New Hampshire and is the favorite in most of the Super Tuesday primaries," Brolin Murphy gleefully announced. "But did you see who came in second in New Hampshire? Not Senator Smith. Not Senator Hunter, who is even older than Uncle Griffin. The person who finished second in New Hampshire because that tiny New England state allows write-in votes was none other than noted Independent and current President Evan Pappas."

Murphy, no doubt, wanted to undercut Johnston while smoothing the way to the presidency for Collins. And the rest of his VOX crew, plus ultra-right wing start-up network NewsCrash, picked up the baton.

But PNT and DVTV took Murphy's baton and ran the other way.

"Maybe President Pappas should run as a Democrat," PNT's Eric James said. "Let's face it. He was lucky to win as an Independent last time. He won't have to be as lucky with Democratic money paving the way."

"Democratic honchos Patricia Paschall and Chuck Shuler are quaking in their boots," DVTV's Ari Melman said. "They are banking on – not that I mean to sound ageist – an old candidate who, and I still don't mean to sound ageist, will be lucky to make it through one term. Meanwhile, there is an Independent candidate out there, an Independent candidate who just happens to be President, who got almost as many votes as Johnston in New Hampshire and who polls well on all of the issues – gun reform, immigration, the economy – that Democrats hold dear."

Thank, God. Not that Melman is trying to make me the Democratic nominee. Thank, God, that Melman – a 50-year-old White man – looks like he might get through an entire show without pandering to what he thinks is his younger audience by trotting out a rap lyric.

And then he trots out a rap lyric.

"If I can drop a few Lil' Wayne bars, 'I'm at the top of the top, but still I climb, and if I should ever fall, the ground will then turn to wine.' If Democrats want to get to the top of the top, yo', maybe they should look up President Pappas. They know where to find him: 1600 Pennsylvania Avenue."

Tarik laughs as I watch it with him.

"Yeah, I know," I say. "Ridiculous."

"His rapping, yes. But you running as a Democrat, not so much."

CHAPTER 35

The decision for Lin is simple. I should tell the world I am bipolar because it would reduce the stigma placed on people suffering from mental illness. Plus, it's the truth. Who knows? Maybe it will help me pick up one vote. Lin will be voting in her first presidential election.

The decision for Ariana isn't as simple. She is an idealist to a point, but also is practical. When she ran a coffee business in Philly, one of her managers wanted to up the dose of coffee per shot. "It's the perfect cup," the manager/coffee artiste told Ariana. But Ariana lost $100,000 one year because of Jose's double-dosing and knew that nobody would get "perfect cups" if Philters went out of business. Jose resigned to pursue coffee perfection elsewhere and Ariana continued to garner Best of Philadelphia awards.

I want to make perfect presidential cups. I also want to stay in business. Ideally, I'd like to make perfect cups while getting enough votes to keep my job, but I don't know if that is possible.

Which is why I've called my new campaign manager, Mary Matin, into the Oval Office this morning. Collins, joined by a growing number of Democrats, have been hammering on this nasty, little 25th amendment thing and I have to respond soon.

"You're what?!" Matin says when I tell her I'm bipolar.

"I've dealt with my bipolar for 30 years and it hasn't stopped me from being a pretty damn good mayor, a better-than-average governor and a good president."

"You won't be a good anything if you go public. You'll be out on your ass."

Matin has headed successful presidential campaigns for both parties. That's why I hired her. I also hired her because she isn't afraid to tell me what she thinks.

"Is there anything else you want to discuss, because I have a meeting with a donor at 11?" Matin says. "You going public with your bipolar is out of the question."

"Tell the donor that you'll be late. Because this is *the* question for me and, last I checked, I still am president."

I discuss all of the medical aspects of bipolar and how I've been able to thrive with it throughout my adult life. Matin brings up my press conference meltdown and the fact that Collins and Johnston are trotting out expert after expert to say that it was something other than a bad reaction to prednisone. I tell her that the press conference was a blip on the radar screen and a good thing long-term because it reminded me of what can happen if I don't follow doctor's orders. I tell her that one of our recent presidents was diagnosed from afar as having narcissistic personality disorder before going out and getting the second-highest vote count in the history of presidential elections.

"But the guy he ran against got the most," Matin says.

Matin mentions Eagleton, dumped by one of the most liberal presidential candidates ever, McGovern, because Eagleton suffered from depression. She brings up George H.W. Bush's physician and his quote that mental illness was "the kiss of death" for a presidential candidate. Obama senior advisor David Axelrod, Matin reminds me, said mental illness would "create a crisis of confidence" in the country.

"Your approval numbers are great, Mr. President," she says. "Why rock the boat?"

"For the greater good."

"Seriously? I thought you were a politician."

"A politician with one of the best campaign managers of all time on the payroll: you. Getting a bipolar president elected in the hands of a lesser campaign manager would be impossible. But you? It will be a piece of cake."

"Wit all due respect, Mr. President, you can't bullshit a bullshitter. And that's what I do for a living. Save your 'greater good' thing for later after you're reelected."

Matin leaves to chat up that donor.

I leave to meet with my Israel – Palestine advisory group, passing Tarik in the hallway.

"What was that all about?" asks Tarik after watching Matin leave the Oval Office.

"Nothing much."

I doubt, though, that the American public would see it that way.

CHAPTER 36

The good thing about campaigning as an incumbent president is that you're always front and center and everything you say is repeated over and over and over again on the evening news. It's a 24-hour-a-day political ad.

But you can't screw up.

Fortunately, I haven't screwed up much since my ill-advised, under-medicated press conference. Early returns on the Israel – Palestine talks are promising. The economy is thriving. We're getting closer to an immigration law that both parties can accept. Infrastructure is, well, infrastructure.

Plus, the Birmingham shooting was the last mass shooting in the U.S. At 47 days, it might set a record for longest period between mass shootings in recent history. Yes, the bar is very, very low. But it's a start and, if the town hall I conducted the other night is an indication, could be a portent of good things to come.

"Everybody for mental health background checks, raise your hands," I started at the University of Kentucky.

Most of the audience, comprised mostly of college students and educators, raised their hands.

"Everybody for banning assault weapons, raise your hands."

Again, most of the audience raised their hands.

"And everybody for prohibiting convicted felons from ever owning a gun, raise your hands."

This one is almost unanimous.

"That was easy," I say. "Kentucky's playing Duke tonight. Big game. Seems like you guys are in a hurry to get back to the dorm to watch it."

Laughs. A good thing. One final question regarding mental health. Not so good.

"Josh Hawler. Senior year. Pre-med. I hate to bring this up, Mr. President, especially because it has nothing to do with guns, but your opponents keep talking about that press conference you gave and invoking the 25th Amendment. I'd like to vote for you, but don't know if I can if you keep having meltdowns. Was it really a reaction to gout medication?"

It's the perfect time for me to come clean. It's the perfect time for me to stop spreading the lie about the prednisone and start spreading the word that a person – me, in this instance – can succeed with a mental illness.

Lin decided to join me at this press conference, and I see her squirming backstage. I don't want to disappoint my daughter. But I also want to win a second term.

"Don't worry. I've switched gout medications," I say.

Later, after hand-shaking and general Presidential schmoozing that took way too much time, Lin and I are in the limo riding back to our hotel.

Lin hasn't spoken to me since she entered the car. She's going back to Northwestern tomorrow, and I don't want what otherwise has been a good two weeks with my daughter to end like this.

"You avoided his question, Dad," Lin finally says.

"But I didn't lie."

Lin doesn't speak to me the rest of the trip and makes sure she is on her way to the airport by the time I wake up the next morning.

My presidential poll numbers are up. My father numbers are way down and it's killing me.

CHAPTER 37

Collins rolls in South Carolina, outdistancing the Republican runner-up by 32 percentage points. Still, Collins' chief "rival" stands in front of a cheering mob later, vows that "we've only just begun," and makes her husband and two beautiful kids act like they believe her.

"How can she do that with a straight face?" I ask Tarik as we watch from the comfort of the Oval Office, a six-pack of beer, chips and guacamole in the vicinity. "I'd respect her more if she got up there and said she didn't have a chance in hell."

"She's running for four years down the road."

"And her poor kids. She makes them complicit in her lie."

I seize up, knowing that I am making Lin complicit in my lie every day that goes by with me not telling the country I'm bipolar.

Johnston wins, too, but his victory celebration looks like my seventh birthday party. Only two kids from the neighborhood showed up, but I was okay with it. More cake for me. The networks aren't okay with Johnston's narrow win over a ragtag field, though, pretty much proclaiming Collins the next President unless the incumbent president – I think I know the guy -- can pull another Independent rabbit out of the hat.

"Let's address the gorilla in the middle of the room," Evan Matthews, one of eight unsmiling DVTV hosts gathered around a way-too-small table, says. "Johnston is too old. Perception matters and, no matter how sharp his people tell us he is, you can't make a 79-year-old pig look like a 50-year-old pig."

"I thought the analogy was about putting lipstick on pigs," Bekka Mornay smiles.

"I guess I'm too old, too."

PNT offers more of the same, calling for the Democrats to nominate a younger, more vibrant candidate before it's too late.

"Or there's President Pappas," Philly boy Jack Tanner says. "Look what he did last time on a shoestring. Think what he'd do this time with all of that Democratic Party money greasing the skids."

"He's his own man," Van Jason says. "It's what people respect about him. He ties himself to the Democrats, he won't be his own man anymore."

Tarik laughs and asks me to pass the chips.

"I sure as hell would respect you less," he says. "But you'd be more likely to get my vote."

"It's a moot point, my man. Patricia Paschall and I have never seen eye-to-eye. And her second-in-command, Chuck Shuler, he's still smarting from that ass-kicking I gave him last election."

Plus, the Democrats never would back a candidate who has announced that he is bipolar and has to take meds every day so he doesn't break into comedy routines every other press conference. Clearly, it is the right political move to stick to my gout story and let the electorate know of my bipolar after the election.

But I'd get my daughter back if I announce now. That means something. Actually, it means a lot, even if I lose the election, move back to West Philly, and hook on with a fancy law firm that will pay big money if I allow them to put my name on their letterhead.

"Oh, hell," Tarik says, downing his fourth beer. Tarik's wisest and certainly most creative political advice always comes after the third beer. "You whupped 'em last time as an Independent. You'll whup them this time as an Independent."

"You really believe that?"

Tarik laughs, spitting out what's left of beer No. 4.

"There are good things about living in West Philly," he says. "Proximity to good cheesesteaks, for one."

CHAPTER 38

Trey Collins must not be worried about his only remaining Republican primary challenger, Nikki Huntley, because he devotes less than a minute of his hour-long sit down with Sean McGill after the South Carolina primary talking about her.

"I have to tell you, Trey," McGill says, "I've had Nikki on my show and she comes across as a genuine, caring person. You must have at least one nice thing you can say about her."

Silence.

"Trey?"

"My momma always taught me, if you don't have anything nice to say about somebody, don't say anything at all."

Trey didn't listen to his momma when he went on to call Griffin Johnston "old" and "ancient" and "doddering."

"But, hey," Collins laughed along with McGill "Old and ancient and doddering have their place...in the Smithsonian."

And Trey certainly didn't heed his momma when he went on a half-hour diatribe about the 25th Amendment and my fitness for president and "the Presidential crisis we face until President Pappas' cabinet convenes and does the right thing: have somebody else run the country."

Collins cites my off-the-rails press conference as McGill tees up footage – I still cringe when I see it – of me making a fool of myself. He also points to my State of the Union address and says a number of psychiatrists have told him that I exhibited manic signs during that talk.

It's what Dr. Carty said after the State of the Union. I have no doubt that Collins has his team of psychiatrists – paid handsomely, no doubt – that he can trot out at a moment's notice.

"He doesn't know what he's talking about," Tarik says.

"Actually, he does."

Collins scoffs at my press conference gout excuse, drawing a few laughs from that damn McGill as Collins gets up from his seat and fakes a limp to a nearby table to get a glass of water.

"Even if he had the gout, and even if his press conference meltdown was caused by a bad reaction to prednisone," he says, "it doesn't' matter. The 25th Amendment allows for the removal of a President who can't conduct the duties of office because of gout, a bad haircut, pretty much anything."

Collins is stooping low, even by Trey Collins standards. But he's playing to his base, a base that thinks every school child above the age of six should be armed with an AK-47, and the Republican Primary is all he has to win at the moment.

Johnston's attack hurts more. I used to respect Griffin, looking up to him when the Pittsburgh-born Senator campaigned for me in my first gubernatorial run. But he's a politician, a politician who is leaking oil in the Democratic primary and has heard whispers about me possibly running as a Democrat.

"I love President Pappas," Johnston says with a straight face in an interview with PNT. "I really do. But I love this country more. And I would hate for this country's fate to rest in the hands of a President – at least, until I win the election – who can't keep his own emotional house in order."

Tarik pours himself a scotch. He pours one for me, too, although he knows I rarely drink and never drink this early in the day

"To your second term," Tarik says, holding his glass up for a toast.

I clink glasses with Tarik, although I don't know where he is going with this.

"Collins is talking about you, not Johnston. Johnston's talking about you, not Collins. You're the person they're worried about and, with all you've accomplished, they have every reason to be scared shitless of the once and future President of the United States."

Tarik, as he has since I faced suspension for allegedly placing a rotten apple on a teacher's desk in fifth grade, is trying to make me feel better. He told me not to worry then and he was right. Tarik told the Lea School principal that he was behind the fruit fiasco. Tarik took the hit and the couple of days off from school that came with it.

Collins and Johnston railing about me shows weakness. It shows fear. It shows that I should be the one who leads the American public four more years, not a couple of cowards who can't campaign on their own merits.

"Aren't you going to get that?" Tarik asks.

I mean, they'd be crazy to vote a gun-toting, Russia-loving lightweight like Collins in and just as crazy to vote for a man clearly showing signs of dementia.

"You want me to get it?"

I snap out of my reverie long enough to hear the phone on my Oval Office desk buzzing.

"What's up, Gladys?"

"It's Vice President Harper. She's waiting out here and says it's urgent."

Weird. I didn't have a meeting scheduled with Shirley.

"Did she say what it's about?"

"Some amendment. The 24th? The 25th? Hey, I'm paid to keep your schedule, not your amendments."

And I'm paid not to violate them.

Collins' rants, I can take. Johnston's, too.

But Shirley? She has the power to convene the cabinet and possibly vote me out of office.

CHAPTER 39

Shirley and I haven't crossed paths since we delivered that talk following the Birmingham shooting.

I have been off doing my president things: trying to get Farid and Noah to focus on peace in the Middle East rather than killing each other, working on new gun control legislation, trying to summon enough energy to focus on an infrastructure bill. Plus, I've been begging Lin for forgiveness. I'd raise her allowance if she was getting one.

Shirley has been off doing her vice-president thing and her vice-president thing is much more difficult, from what I hear, than the vice-president things my predecessor presidents gave their seconds-in-command. She chairs my Civil Rights task force and has managed to get parties from both sides to make headway, although you wouldn't know it from cable news stations that choose to stick to their agendas rather than the facts. She has held two town halls on infrastructure – maybe I should foist this bill on her – and was the commencement speaker for her daughter's Bethune-Cookman graduating class.

"Have you been avoiding me?" I ask after Shirley takes a seat. "You don't call. You don't write. What's a president to do?"

"I wish I could have avoided this," she says. "Unfortunately, the noise from both sides of the aisle has gotten too loud and I'm the one who has to take charge."

Shirley goes on to say that she believes I have been handling my duties as President wonderfully, that she is proud to serve as my vice president, that the best political move she ever made was accepting the invitation to join my ticket for the last election. Shirley adds that she hopes to be with me every step along the way for the next election.

"I sense a 'but' coming," I say.

The 'but,' I know, is the outcry to use the 25th Amendment to kick me out of the White House.

"It's politics, Shirley. You know that. They want to win. They don't give a damn about the Constitution."

Shirley reaches for the tissue box on the table by her seat. I've seen the woman control her emotions while talking to mothers of soldiers slain overseas. And she didn't shed a tear during that last, glorious election night when we shocked the world and became the first Independent pairing ever to win the White House.

But she is wiping away a tear now.

"I don't have many friends, Mr. President," she says.

"Evan."

"There's a reason I don't have many friends. I've spent most of my life trying to get ahead because, well, that's just the way things are when you grow up poor and Black in Alabama. I was so busy studying that I didn't spend much time learning how to relate to people."

"We relate."

"We do. That's what I told Senator Collins when he asked me to convene the Cabinet for a 25th Amendment vote. That's what I told Senator Johnston. I asked – no, begged – for them to get somebody impartial, maybe the Secretary of State, to convene a 25th Amendment hearing."

"The Secretary of State doesn't like me?"

"He's impartial. But they wanted it to be me. It's in the Constitution and my duty is to uphold the Constitution, even if upholding the Constitution means doing something I don't like."

"What did I ever do to the Secretary of State?"

Shirley laughs. I wasn't joking, though. I don't know whether to exclude the Secretary of State from our next White House poker game or to plot some kind of cheating strategy with Tarik to take all his money.

I sit next to Shirley and put my arm around her.

"You do what you have to do, Shirley. I mean it. As much as I respected you before today, I respect you more now. We'll still be friends, no matter what happens."

Shirley brushes away another tear, heads toward the door and turns around.

"The Cabinet hearing is in two weeks, Mr. President."

And she's gone.

And then she's back, peaking in just before I can down a shot of Jack Daniels.

"For what it's worth, Mr. President, I'm rooting for you."

CHAPTER 40

I'm back in the Oval Office the next morning after spending the rest of the day working off my 25th Amendment angst by shooting hoops with Tarik, having a candlelight dinner with Ariana and watching three reruns of "Seinfeld."

The Washington Guardian, New York Beacon and Philadelphia Journal are in front of me, one of the cable news commentators is squawking on the TV behind me and the still-unsigned infrastructure bill sits off to the side of the desk. Now, I have another excuse to procrastinate about the bill: I could be drummed out of office in two weeks.

"They'd never kick you out of office," Ariana says, finishing up her coffee before she heads off to give a talk to the Women's Entrepreneur Association. "You're doing too well."

"Doing well might be important to those people you're talking to today. In politics, not so much."

My staff will be here in an hour. I really should spend a minute or two on the infrastructure bill because that's what we'll spend most of our time talking about this morning. But I've been reading the Philadelphia Journal — the Phils pitcher tossed a no-hitter last night — and some of the Guardian and Beacon.

My phone buzzes.

"Senators Paschall and Shuler are here," Gladys says. "What should I tell them?"

I look at the half-finished Phillies story. The 14th no-hitter in Phillies history. Damn, I want to finish that and the two sidebars accompanying the main story.

"Show them in."

Paschall and Shuler, Chief of the Intelligence Committee, are all smiles, which wasn't the case at the beginning of my term. The Democrats thought they had the last election in the bag until I threw my hat in the ring. They blamed me for siphoning votes from Shuler, who still holds a grudge while also holding one of the most powerful positions in the Senate.

Hell, I would have been content to keep plugging away as Governor of Pennsylvania but Shuler's primary rival, Bernie Sans, was too strident on just about every issue and would have been just as divisive as the Republican candidate. I wanted to inject a bit of sanity into presidential politics when I entered the fray, but Sans soon dropped out of the race, Shuler was hit with a paternity suit after winning the Democratic nomination and the Republican nominee continued to ridicule the handicapped, women, Blacks and just about everybody who votes. The guy's campaign advisor, I suspected, was working for the Democrats. But, no, he did dumb all on his own and an Independent – me – eked out a win.

And here I am today with the leader of the Senate and Shuler sitting in front of me at an ungodly time for senators. What do they want?

"Patricia, Chuck, always good to see you," I stand, shake their hands and try to act like I meant what I just said. "But I'm meeting with my staff about infrastructure – do one of you guys want to handle it? -- in a little bit and don't have much time."

"This won't take much time," Paschall says.

Paschall talks about my "misguided" views on criminal justice reform, my "pie-in-the-sky" views about the economy and my "failure" to come out strongly enough on gun control. I don't mention that Paschall would have all citizens, and possibly police officers, armed with water guns.

"Hell, Patricia," I say, "At least two of the three major cable stations probably were saying that this morning. You didn't come all the way to the Oval Office to tell me that."

Shuler goes on to tell me that he is shocked at how well I am doing even though he should be the one sitting in my seat.

"I'm just warming it for you, Chuck. You'll get 'em next time. Or the time after that."

Shuler says he is surprised by how well I have adapted to Beltway politics in my first term. He credits me for lessening the bickering between Republicans and Democrats to a dull roar. He talks about progress on environmental issues, education, the Supreme Court nominee I trotted out last month and the Middle East.

"I could have heard that on cable news, too, Chuck," I say.

Paschall looks at Shuler. Shuler looks at Paschall. Who wants to get to the point, if there actually is a point?

"We want you to run for president again," Paschall says.

"I planned to."

"As a Democrat," Shuler says.

This, I wasn't expecting.

"We have one condition," Paschall says before she walks out the door with Shuler. "You have to debate Johnston. We think he's slipping, but we could be wrong. Before you get our support, you'll have to show on national TV next Tuesday that you're the right man for the job."

I could tell Paschall and Shuler about the 25th Amendment hearing, which Paschall and Schuler don't know about yet.

If they want to throw Democratic money my way — and they won't if Johnston mops the floor with me — who am I to turn it down?

CHAPTER 41

You always remember your first presidential debate even when that debate is held at a small college, televised by an obscure local television station and your opponents are not well-known nationally.

My first presidential debate was held four years ago at LaSalle, a small school in North Philadelphia. The local PBN affiliate, known more for its long and boring documentaries than its ratings, televised it. Ralph Naper of the Consumer Party and Jill Jones of the Green Party were up on the debate stage with me, all of us trying to grab enough attention to garner an outside shot in the presidential election against the Republican and Democratic nominees.

"We're going for a soundbite here," Tarik told me before I took the stage. "If you think it's outrageous, use it. It will make national news."

Naper's campaign manager must have told him the same thing because the Consumer Party candidate came out with something catchy, if not outrageous. The problem for Naper was that it was catchy way back in 1928 when it was the rallying cry for Great Depression President Herbert Hoover.

"A chicken in every pot!" Naper exclaimed early in the debate.

The silence in the crowd was deafening.

Jones' "sound bite" may have been worse.

"Green is the new black!" the Green Party candidate shouted as students in the audience turned to each other, no doubt wondering what

Jones was talking about. My best guess: *Orange is the New Black* was a popular TV series at the time and Jones figured she would piggyback on the show's popularity. She didn't.

I waited until I delivered my last remarks.

"Go Eagles!" I screamed to the Philadelphia crowd. I had to wait a minute before the ovation died down. "And, what the hell, go Cowboys! I have to win Texas to have a shot at this thing, guys."

The Cowboys remark drew deafening boos. No matter. My remark, the cheers I got for the Eagles comment and the boos I got for the Cowboys comment made national news.

* * *

Tonight at Moorehouse College, I will become one of the few sitting presidents in U.S. history to take part in a primary debate. The reason is simple. Most sitting presidents run unopposed or don't want to risk big leads before the general election. But I'm trying to gain the backing of the Democratic Party and have to out-debate Griffin Johnston to get it.

"Just don't fuck up," Tarik tells me before I take the stage.

Johnston's opening remarks are impressive, although I put on my best poker face to mask how impressive I think he is. He has been a U.S. Senator for 35 years, probably should have been elected President 12 years ago and is adored by the American public for his folksy, self-effacing demeanor.

"I'm just a poor kid from Pittsburgh," Johnston starts. He spent the rest of his time talking about his loving wife, his loving children and his desire to buck the trend and run a clean, uplifting campaign.

How do you counter a man who loves his wife, loves his children and wants to run a clean, uplifting campaign? I'll go high against a man who supported me in my run for Pennsylvania governor.

Paschall and Shuler want me to go low, though. They want me to pound on Johnston's age and his dwindling mental capacity.

The hell with them.

"Before I talk about myself," I start, "and you've heard me talk about myself a lot over the last four years, I want to talk about Senator Griffin Johnston."

I don't know if my opening statement is confusing Griffin or if that is his normal expression.

"I got into politics because of this guy. Thirty years ago, I'm shuffling paper in the Philadelphia mayor's office and my current chief of staff and lifelong friend, Tarik Taylor, tells me I'd make a good governor. I never listened to Tarik growing up and I wouldn't have listened to him then. But I got a call from Griffin Johnston, a Senator at the time, and I sure as hell listened to him. Ariana and I had dinner with Griffin and Jane, Griffin convinced me that we'd make a good Pennsylvania tag team with him as senator and me as governor, and I threw my hat in the ring. I'll always be thankful to Griffin for that, although I'm guessing Senator Collins – with all of the nasty things he's been saying on TV about me these days – isn't so thankful."

I finish by ticking off my accomplishments and draw a smattering of applause. I'm guessing that Paschall and Schiff aren't clapping. They wanted me to take Johnston to the woodshed, but I can't do it against a guy I respect.

DVTV host and erstwhile rapper Ari Melman starts the questioning.

"That decision you made thirty years ago – convincing President Pappas to run for Governor – would you still make it, Senator Johnston?"

"Of course," Johnston says. "With President Pappas in the Governor's office, I'd be a shoo-in for the White House."

The crowd laughs. Melman doesn't. Ari has spent the last week hammering on my fitness for the presidency, bringing on "expert" psychiatrists to discuss the issue, and wants Johnston to go there.

Johnston hesitates after Melman presses him with another question. And then he goes there.

"Let's assume that President Pappas' performance at the press conference was caused by a bad reaction to prednisone," Johnston says. "Or let's assume that President Pappas' performance was occasioned by the mania a number of mental health experts believe it to be. It really doesn't matter. The 25th Amendment allows for the removal of a president because he can't perform his duties. And President Pappas, whether it's gout or bipolar or a bad oyster...."

More laughs.

"...has shown that he can't perform his duties."

Should I play the senility card? Collins has played it against Johnston. Paschall and Shuler want me to play it against Johnston. Arguably, it might even be the moral thing to do. This country certainly deserves a leader who isn't senile.

But I can't play it and live with myself at the same time.

"FDR was saddled to a wheelchair and was one of the great presidents of all time," I say. "Thank God, Congress didn't take away his presidency before FDR took away Adolph Hitler's campaign to rule the world."

"You're no FDR, Mr. President," Johnston says.

Griffin should know. I think he and FDR were contemporaries. *Don't go there, Evan.*

"And you're not Harry Truman or JFK," Johnston continues, "or Hillary Clinton or any of the other great Democratic Presidents who followed FDR."

Hillary Clinton didn't follow anybody as president. Uh, oh.

"The only reason we're having this debate is that the powers that be in the Democratic Party don't think I have, for lack of a clinical term, all my marbles," Johnston continues. "And they think this guy up on stage with me, a guy I once backed for dogcatcher sheriff has more marbles...."

It wasn't sheriff, Griffin. Can someone please save Johnston before he further tarnishes his political legacy?

"Um....uh. What was I saying?" Johnston continues.

Titters from the audience.

"I was a great marble player when I was growing up. I, uh, um...and checkers. I loved that game."

Then silence.

From Johnston.

From the audience.

And then more laughter. I can't take this.

"Enough!" I scream.

I rush over to Johnston.

"Are you okay, buddy?"

"What did I do?"

"Let's get you backstage to Jane. She's waiting for you."

That was the end of the debate.

That was the end of Griffin Johnston's political career.

CHAPTER 42

Paschall and Shuler are waiting outside the Oval Office the next day looking way too happy for my tastes.

"We're going to kick ass in November," Shuler says.

Yeah, just like I kicked yours four Novembers ago.

"It's a shame what happened to Griffin last night," Paschall says. "He was a good man."

"He *is* a good man," I say.

Paschall and Schiff fill me in on their plans. I still have two nominal candidates running against me, but Paschall says the Democratic party has a few attack ads run through PACs that will turn this into a one-horse race very quickly.

"No attack ads," I say.

"You're on the Democratic team now," Paschall says. "Plus, a PAC wants to run something, we can't stop them."

Yeah, right.

They also have a new campaign manager lined up for me. Jackman Bown has run successful campaigns for two Presidents and is going for the trifecta. I already have a campaign manager, Mary Matin, and Paschall tells me I can keep her on as an assistant to Bown.

"She won't go for that," I say.

"She has to."

I feel a weight lifted off my shoulders when Paschall and Shuler leave the room. Yes, I have a better chance of winning with the Democratic machinery leveling the playing field. Yes, I won't have to run on a shoestring budget that probably wouldn't have been enough to beat Collins in November, assuming I get past this 25th Amendment business. And, yes, it will be nice standing onstage at the Democratic Convention, the band playing, streamers and confetti streaming down as Ariana showers me with kisses and Lin looks adoringly into my eyes as millions of TV viewers look on.

There was no Independent convention four years ago, just Tarik saying, "I'll buy you a beer," after I told him I was running against the Republicans and Democrats.

PNT already has the news courtesy, I'm sure, of Paschall and Shuler: "So, it will be President Pappas vs. Senator Collins in November," Jack Tanner announces. "And for Senator Griffin Johnston, my hat's off to you, sir. You were a good man."

He *is* a good man, damn it. Note to self: introduce a bill increasing funding for Alzheimer's research. It's nice that people are living longer these days. It would be even nicer if they were living longer *and* better.

DVTV: "Damn, I wish I laid a bet in Vegas a week ago," Melman says. "I would have gotten good odds on President Pappas. Winning as an Independent last time was a miracle. But winning as a Democrat won't be as tough or, as Tupac said...."

I turn off the TV. I have better things to do. That infrastructure bill still is sitting on my desk and tackling it is a better alternative than listening to Melman or Tanner or any of the pundits delivering Johnston post-mortems.

I'll visit Griffin later. Hopefully, he won't blame me for what went down.

Which is when all hell breaks loose. Tarik breaks into the room, my phone starts ringing off the hook and I hear ambulances outside.

"There's been another mass shooting, a big mass shooting," Tarik says.

"Where?"

"Look outside your window."

CHAPTER 43

ut I can't see outside the window with all of the smoke.

"Get my car ready," I tell Gladys. "And have the Secret Service detail standing by."

The shooting, I learn, took place at Temple Beth Shalom, five blocks from the White House. Jacob Platner and Ruth Weiselberg would have taken their vows at 11 that morning and danced the hora at the Arlington Country Club later that afternoon if a shooter hadn't broken into the synagogue and killed 123 people and injuring 213 before detonating a suicide bomb to take his own life.

The would-be bride and groom are dead. The would-be groom's father, Republican Senator Morris Platner, is one of the injured. Police aren't calling it a hate crime even though the shooter screamed "Allahu Akbar" before opening fire.

I can hear senators and congressmen chiming in already. *Thoughts and prayers, thoughts and prayers, thoughts and prayers.* How many times have I heard the same thing, the same damn thing, after all of the mass shootings that have snuffed out so many innocent lives in what is supposed to be the greatest country in the world.

After the gnashing of teeth, if this follows the script of other mass shootings, there will be town halls, which will lead to calls for gun reform, which will lead to proposed laws that won't even scratch the murdering surface but will make politicians feel good about themselves and, more importantly, make their constituents feel good about the politicians when it's time to vote.

"What do you have, Chief?" I ask. D.C. Police Chief Sean Murphy, FBI director James Comer, CIA director James Inger and other members of the D.C. metro force and the FBI are hunkered down in the Oval Office after I return from the scene of the crime.

"Jawad Bahir, 23, Islamic Jihad," Murphy says. "He posted on the web last week that he was going to do something big, something to disrupt peace in the Middle East and strike a blow for Palestinians. He was the shooter."

"And we didn't do anything about the threat?"

"We questioned him, but his story checked out and the post looked like it came from outside the country. We secured the wedding anyway. Or, at least, we thought we secured it."

I'm worried about a bomb going off in Gaza City or Jerusalem, blowing up all of the work Noah, Farid and I put into peace talks, and a terrorist strikes five blocks away from the White House. Five blocks away from the White House! If this murderer — and that's what he is; not a freedom-fighter or whatever euphemism they give people who murder for a cause these days — certainly knew how to send a number of messages:

No peace in the Middle East as long as there is an Israel.

Free the Palestinians.

From the river to the sea.

But maybe I'm getting ahead of myself. Maybe this was a lone killer, a lone, mentally ill killer who had nothing better to do with his time than commit mass murder. Maybe this isn't about peace in the Middle East. Maybe it was about him getting fired from a job and deciding to lash out at his boss by lashing out the way anti-Semites have been lashing out throughout history.

"You have a phone call," Gladys buzzes in.

"Can it wait? I have a lot to go over with the police and FBI."

"I think you'll want to take this."

I do. It's Farid.

"Intifada had nothing to do with it," he says.

"The shooter said he was Islamic Jihad."

"I've dealt with Islamic Jihad. It's not them, either."

No sooner do I hang up with Farid, Noah calls.

"Things were going so well," he says. "And then this happens."

"Farid says it has nothing to do with Intifada. And I believe him."

"I want to believe him. I don't know if I do."

I promise to get back to Noah, as I promised to get back to Farid.

For now, there are details of the shooting to be discussed, press conferences to convene and thoughts and prayers – real thoughts and prayers – to be made.

And there's a side trip to be made. Senator Platner is at Cedar Sinai. He's been one of my chief critics in the Senate, but I want to see if he's okay.

CHAPTER 44

First, though, there is prep for the 25th Amendment hearing just over a week away. I'll visit Senator Platner later after the smoke -- literally -- has cleared.

Tarik is playing the role of Secretary of State James Mason, the lone cabinet holdover from the previous administration. Mason has been helpful with relationships that he formed under the previous president but, for the most part, has been a pain in my ass. He didn't want me to meet with the Palestinians and Israelis. He didn't want me to broker a trade deal with Russia last year. He didn't want me to engage in a cultural exchange with China two years ago, telling me that I would look "weaker than that light beer piss you drink."

Mason, I believe, has wanted me out of the White House for a long time. Next week, he might get his wish.

"Be nice to me," I tell Tarik as we wait for the other "cabinet members" to arrive.

"Mason won't be nice to you."

"You're right. Hit me with your best shot."

Curtain is playing Shirley, who will run the 25th Amendment meeting and ultimately decide whether to send the Cabinet's findings to Congress. Jim Banoff will play the Secretary of Defense who, according to one of my moles in his office, thinks I should spend less time negotiating with the Palestinians and more time bombing them.

Staff members playing the Secretary of the Interior, the Secretary of Homeland Security and various other secretaries file in one by one. The real Secretary of the Interior is on my side, the Secretary of Homeland Security wants me deported and there's a split among my other Cabinet members, my sources tell me.

Figuratively, there's another person in the room. It's Lin. I know how she wants me to handle the 25th Amendment meeting – come clean with my bipolar – but I can't bring myself to listen to her even though it could mean an extension of the cold war between us.

"That gout, boy, it makes you do all kinds of crazy things," Tarik, as Secretary of State, starts his questioning. "Actually, Mr. President, it doesn't. It just makes you limp. That ain't crazy. Do you really expect us to believe that shit your press secretary has been trotting out? Because it doesn't play with me, and the American public isn't as dumb as you seem to think it is."

"Gout isn't anything to laugh at, Mr. Secretary," I say. "Hell, my Chief of Staff – Tarik Taylor – wipes the basketball floor with me every time I have it."

"You wanted me to be serious, but you can joke?" Tarik asks.

"I'm the President."

"Not for long if you don't take this seriously."

Jim Banoff is up next. He writes a good speech. Let's see if he asks a good question.

"Let's assume it was gout and prednisone," Banoff says. "What's to stop you from losing it when you are involved in intense negotiations with Russia, China, your Middle Eastern friends, if you're battling gout?"

"I won't take prednisone."

"And you'll experience intense pain. The 25th Amendment provides that a president shall be removed when he is unable to discharge the duties of the presidency. Are you telling us that you would be able to discharge your duties while you are experiencing excruciating pain?"

Jim is having too much fun.

"Hell, I read that speech Jim Banoff gave me word-for-word the other night. You think gout is painful? Banoff ended three sentences with prepositions and inserted a 'be that as it may' in there somewhere. I sounded like an elitist tool."

"Still trying to get laughs," Tarik says. He's not laughing. He is pissed. "Are you gunning for a standup career and a couple of HBO specials."

Hmmm. It might not be a bad idea.

"Anybody else?" I ask.

Silence.

"Anybody? Come on, guys, the future of this country is at stake. Not to mention the future of my employment."

Why don't you tell them the truth?

Where did that come from?

The truth. You're bipolar. You take meds for it. It doesn't mean you can't be a good president. It just means it will be tougher winning a second term if the country knows.

"Mr. President." It's Aida/Shirley.

Maybe Lin's right.

"Mr. President? You seem a bit preoccupied. Is it the synagogue shooting, because we can do this another time."

Maybe I should come clean with my bipolar.

"Mr. President?"

I snap out of my reverie.

"Yeah. The synagogue. We'll do this another time. And thanks, Tarik. I can't help myself sometimes. That's why you'll be at the hearing. Kick me under the table if I say something stupid."

"No doubt you'll say something stupid. Hopefully, my aim is good and I kick the right person."

CHAPTER 45

The head nurse on the seventh floor at Cedar Sinai tells me I have 15 minutes.

"But I'm the President of the United States," I say.

"And I'm the head nurse," she says. "On this floor, I outrank you."

I try to negotiate – hey, it worked with Farid and Noah – but all I get after telling her that I can score Washington Nationals tickets or dinner at a swanky D.C. restaurant is this:

"You're down to 10 minutes. Try to be quick, although I've seen you on TV and know that's not your strong suit."

I've come to visit Senator Platner bearing a gift. And it's not just any gift. During earlier, less contentious times, Senator Platner and Democratic Senator Ramon Rivas co-sponsored an energy bill and we cracked open a bottle of Chivas Regal XII in my office to celebrate the signing, the fact that it was bipartisan and, most importantly, to enjoy ourselves.

"Damn good scotch," Platner said then. "And, coming from an Orthodox Jew who doesn't touch the stuff, that is the highest compliment."

It also may have been the last compliment I ever got from Morris Platner. We've sparred over taxes. He thinks I tax too much; I think he wants to let his rich cronies off the hook. We've sparred over gun control. He thinks I want to eliminate the Second Amendment; I think he values the Second Amendment over the First. And, lately, we have sparred over the Middle East peace talks.

The press, with very few exceptions, have lauded the peace talks. Platner, at the risk of losing votes in a liberal state that somehow has voted him in four straight terms, thinks they are a big mistake.

"Ah," Morris says as I enter the room. "A Greek bearing gifts."

"You couldn't come up with a better line than that?"

"On the amount of morphine I'm on? You're lucky I just don't drool on you."

Nurse Ratchet, standing nearby as I approach Morris' bed, says it's okay if I share a drink with my erstwhile Senate nemesis.

"It might even ease his pain. And, oh, you're down to five minutes," she says and leaves the room.

I truly feel sorry for Morris, watching his hand shaking as he lifts the glass of scotch to his lips. He is one of the lions of the Senate, a man who looks 6-feet on TV and seems like he is 6-foot-6 when he is lecturing me on the problems of this bill or that bill. But he is 5-foot-7 and looks like every other patient forced to wear dehumanizing hospital gowns.

"L'chaim," Morris says, raising his glass.

"Steen ee-ya sas," I respond, summoning what little Greek I know to echo Morris' sentiment.

Morris motions me closer, and I sit next to his bed. From accounts I have seen on the news, he has had a steady stream of visitors today. Senator Collins made the splashiest appearance, managing to insinuate himself onto all of the major cable news programs of the day wishing Senator Platner a speedy recovery just before blasting me for what he calls my naive attempt to bring the Palestinians and Israelis together.

"President Pappas isn't paying for it, though," Collins said to Brolin Murphy. "But my friend, Morris Platner, is. I don't know whether he will live or die. I do know that his son, Jacob Platner, won't get a chance to marry the woman he loved."

Paschall and Shuler also paid tribute, along with senators from both sides of the aisle. Some, I'm sure, are truly sorry. Others, I'm equally certain, are doing it for the photo op.

But this isn't a photo op for me. Only two Secret Service agents, both waiting in the hospital reception area, know about this.

"I appreciate the visit," Morris says as I move close enough to hear. "And I appreciate the scotch. I'm a little foggy now, but I still remember when we cracked a bottle in better – much better – times."

"Thank you, Morris."

"I'd hold the thanks," he says, motioning me closer.

I am not ready for what I get when I bend closer to Morris.

He throws what is left of his glass of scotch in my face.

"My son is dead," he whispers. "You don't negotiate with terrorists. Now, get the hell out of here."

CHAPTER 46

One-hundred, twenty-three dead, two-hundred thirteen injured in Washington synagogue massacre.

That is the headline in the New York Beacon the next day.

Senator's son dies; Senator Platner in critical condition.

That is the headline in the Washington Guardian, which is on my Oval Office desk with a dozen or so papers the next day. The Guardian and Beacon stuck with the facts, but other newspapers took it further.

USA News: **Palestinian nationalist guns down over 300, takes own life in synagogue shooting.**

The New York Telegram: **Was massacre revenge for peace talks? Is President responsible?**

"The killer was a lone wolf," Tarik says, stalking my office like a caged tiger. "A lone, fucking, insane wolf. He wouldn't have been able to spell Gaza if you spotted him the 'G' and the 'Z.'"

"And the Telegram wouldn't have been able to sell as many papers if you spotted them the truth," I say.

My mind is with the dead and with Senator Platner, despite his waste of perfectly good scotch on my face. I'm alive. Senator Platner's son isn't, and Morris is in critical condition.

But I can't help wondering if the peace talks, something I truly – maybe naively – thought could end the bloodshed in the Middle East, may have ended.

It doesn't take long for my worries to be confirmed. I turn on VOX and there's Brolin Murphy, sitting with two leading Republicans, wondering the same thing.

"President Pappas' intentions were good," Senator Chernowitz, one of the Republican moderates says. "But the execution, well, a number of presidents have tried and failed in the Middle East before."

"We assume his intentions were good," Senator Hawman interrupts. "Or his intentions might have more to do with winning a second term."

What? Over 300 injured or killed yesterday and Hawman already is turning this into a political football?

PNT is kinder. Barely.

"Here's what we know," Jack Tanner says. "One, this is the worst mass shooting in U.S. history. Two, the gunman was Palestinian. And, three, the shooting took place at a synagogue and most of the victims were Jewish. Here's what we don't know: was the shooting a reprisal for President Pappas' Palestine – Israel talks?"

Tanner struggles through his newscast. He has been one of the biggest proponents of the peace talks, having reported on so many Israeli deaths over the years, and clearly can envision a treaty meant to save lives falling apart.

Join the club, Jack.

DVTV usually is in my corner. But they run the most damning sound bite of all late in the afternoon.

"You don't negotiate with terrorists," Senator Platner says from his hospital bed, repeating the line he used after he threw his drink in my face. "But that's what President Pappas did. And I couldn't dance at my son's wedding."

Tarik shuts off the TV.

"Damn him," Tarik says.

"He lost a son."

"But he doesn't know if this has anything to do with the peace talks."

"He lost a son."

"Well, you better do some damage control."

I will, starting with a press conference on the White House lawn later.

For now, my heart is with Morris and all of the families who lost loved ones during what was supposed to be a joyous occasion.

But it wasn't my fault. That's what I keep telling myself. I also keep telling myself that I was trying to do good, that the shooting had nothing to do with the treaty I am negotiating with Noah and Farid, that FBI and police investigations will reveal that this was the work of one person, not an organized group bent on the destruction of Israel.

That's what I keep telling myself. At some point I might even believe it.

CHAPTER 47

Emma Casserly is a good person, a very good person, who has served the 26th Congressional District in New York well for 22 years. Casserly decided to run in the Democratic primaries, though, and must be regretting her decision now.

An ad, sponsored by the Democrats Against Racism, came out last night accusing Casserly of calling someone a "Black buffoon" in a social media post 10 years ago. Casserly vehemently denied it. The woman Casserly allegedly attacked vehemently denied it. But there it was, in big letters on TV, the racially offensive term with Casserly's smiling face next to it.

"You know, they can doctor those posts," Tarik tells me.

"Please don't tell me you ever doctored a post to get me elected," I say.

"Okay. I won't tell you."

The truth doesn't matter in politics these days. Casserly wasn't doing well against Johnston before the ad ran. I doubt she will last much longer in the Democratic primary and will return to New York with a tarnished reputation when she bows out.

"One down, one to go," Tarik says.

"Don't tell me you're taking pleasure in this."

"Okay. I won't tell you."

South Dakota Senator Larry Marchand was hanging on by his fingernails against Johnston before Johnston dropped out. He better grow longer fingernails, I'm thinking, after an ad thrown together by Democrats for

Women's Rights runs the day after the Casserly hatchet job.

"Senator Marchand says he is for women's rights," the ad starts. You know this isn't going to be pretty when you hear the foreboding music and see the shadowy black and white background with Marchand's hazy figure looming. "But Marchand sponsored a bill in 1982 that would have restricted a woman's right to choose to four weeks. And he sponsored another bill in 1984 that would have imprisoned doctors who performed abortions."

Marchand threatened to sue Democrats for Women's Rights the next day. I'm guessing that he won't be able to find them or will find a bankrupt shell corporation of a shell corporation within a shell corporation. You can't get blood from a stone, and you definitely can't get money from a shell corporation that may or may not have existed and may or may not have money.

You also can't completely regain your reputation once one of these attack ads runs. I know. I was the target of an attack ad during my gubernatorial campaign and my lead was vanishing until it came out that the author of the ad was none other than the person I was running against.

"Congrats," Tarik says after viewing the Marchand ad. "You're the last Democratic primary candidate standing."

"I wanted to win fair and square."

"Cut the boy scout shit. You want me to tell you about all the dirty shit I pulled to get you where you are today?"

"No."

"Okay, I won't tell you."

So, I'm going to be the Democratic nominee barring a phoenix-like return from the dead by Casserly or Marchand or another candidate who has the cojones to run against a sitting president with truckloads of Democratic money behind him.

I'll stil have to fend off attacks about the synagogue killings despite the

FBI's initial reports that the gunman acted alone, no claims by a jihadist group taking credit and my well-received remarks at Temple Beth Shalom, where the shooting took place.

I also have to survive that nasty little 25th Amendment hearing that will start at noon tomorrow. Hopefully, though, everything that is said at the hearing stays in the hearing.

"They're not kicking you out because you have gout," Tarik says.

"No, they won't. But I don't have it now. Want to shoot hoop."

"I thought you'd never ask."

CHAPTER 48

o I sit at the head of the table like I usually do, or do I don a prison jumpsuit and allow armed guards to escort me out of these august chambers in handcuffs?"

Tarik kicks me under the table. This thing just started and I already screwed up.

It's just after noon on the day that could start the 25th Amendment ball rolling and I sit with Vice President Harper and members of my Cabinet in the James Monroe Room.

I thought a little gallows humor would be a good way to start. It wasn't, and I have a bruise on my leg to prove it.

"Mr. President," Harper says, "none of us wants to be here. But your actions during your gout press conference and your actions at previous press conferences and speeches have brought your ability to run this country under question. This is a serious matter. All of the people in this room take it as such. It is imperative that you do, too."

"*As such*?" Shirley really is serious and, looking at the faces of my Secretary of State, my Secretary of Defense and all of the other secretaries I appointed, all of them are just as serious.

Section 4 of the 25th Amendment never has been invoked, although the country came close during Ronald Reagan's second term when members of Reagan's staff thought he might be suffering from Alzheimer's. Chief of Staff Howard Baker said Reagan was fine, though, and one of the most popular presidents in this country's history stayed on to complete his second term.

Where is Howard Baker when I need him? I like Shirley, but she stands to benefit most if the people in this room determine that I am unfit to continue as president. Shirley would submit a recommendation to Congress and Congress would vote on whether I should stay. If I go, the country will have its first Black female president – too long coming, in my opinion – in history.

"Hopefully, we can finish this in one day, Mr. President," Harper says. "But we are prepared to convene for as long as it takes. No witnesses have been called today, but they are standing at the ready if your testimony and the testimony of others in this room isn't sufficient to make a determination."

It will take more than one day, I know, to change the minds of the people in this room who want me out of the White House. It might take weeks, in fact. That wouldn't be good for the country, good for negotiations in the Middle East or good for my current standing as presumptive nominee for the Democratic Party."

"Tell us about that press conference, Mr. President," Secretary of State Mason starts. Mason was one of the best trial lawyers in the country before I named him Secretary of State. I might have picked somebody else if I knew he'd be questioning me in a life-and-death political struggle one day. "Tell us how often you are stricken with gout, how often you take prednisone for the gout and how often – if ever – you have experienced mania after taking prednisone for the gout."

Mason is operating from the information my staff, on my orders, presented to the public. Only Tarik, Ariana, Lin, Dr. Carty and I know that my erratic press conference was a result of me not taking my bipolar meds. But Mason and the rest of the politicians, save for a few of my detractors in Congress, believe my gout excuse. At least, I think they believe it.

Lin isn't a politician. But she didn't believe me then and she would be disgusted by the written remarks I have prepared for Mason and the rest of the cabinet today. She told me to come forward with my bipolar when I was running for President four years ago. She told me to come forward with my bipolar after I was elected. And she wants me to come forward with my bipolar today.

Ah, the innocence of youth. I was robbed of some of it when I slept with Jenny Smith in the 10th grade. And I was robbed of the rest of it when I decided to get into politics.

Lin will forgive me. But there are bigger things at stake here – keeping the future of the country out of the hands of Trey Collins, for one – than telling the truth.

Or maybe Lin won't forgive me. She is one of the most principled people I know, certainly more principled than me as I stand here ready to continue with the gout lie. She suffers from generalized anxiety disorder herself and knows that having a U.S. President with bipolar would alleviate some of the stigma attached to mental illness.

No, she'll forgive me. I hope so, anyway. At least, Ariana will forgive me. We've talked about this, and she also thinks it is crucial that I remain as president even if I have to tell a white lie.

White? Will Lin forgive me? Will she hold it against me? I can tell everybody I have bipolar and win. No, I can't. Yes, I can. But Lin....but, a second term...

Fuck it.

"It wasn't the gout, everyone," I say, stuffing my prepared remarks back in my pocket. "I have bipolar disorder."

CHAPTER 49

The 25th Amendment meeting was supposed to be secret. At least, that was the plan. Why worry the public with something as inconsequential as gout when there are plenty of other issues to worry about?

I turn on my TV when I get back to the White House that night and find that the initial plan lasted about as long as my hopes for the coq au vin Ariana promised me. She is out with Lin, who is on break from Northwestern. And a president with bipolar is more newsworthy than a guy who hobbles around a bit.

"I have all the respect in the world for people who battle mental illness daily," Trey Collins is saying to Brolin Murphy on VOX. "But I don't have respect for someone who tried to hide his illness by telling us it was gout. And I have concern, grave concern, for a country that is being led by a man who we trust to keep the peace but can't keep his own peace of mind."

Who leaked this? My money is on my Secretary of State, the cabinet member I consider least loyal to me. Or it could be the person who has the most to gain if the 25th Amendment ended my presidency. My Vice President, I believe, truly is a good person. But she truly is a politician, and politicians tend to make decisions that further their careers. Or it could be my Secretary of the Interior. I really don't know.

"Bipolar can be controlled," Anthony Forrest, the head of the Mental Health Association is telling Bekka Mornay on DVTV. "Take your meds, exercise, get your rest and you're as good to go as anybody else in the general population."

Forrest is great. Note to self: extend an offer as head of cabinet post if I get through this.

"Nearly 50 percent of U.S. presidents have had mental illness," Forrest tells PNT's Jonathan Price later that night. "And we're talking serious mental illness. Severe depression. Bipolar disorder. Anxiety disorder. It stands to reason. The job of President of the United States might be the most stressful job in the world. With all that stress, I suspect that the percentage of presidents who have had to deal with mental illness is even higher than reported."

But I have been battling bipolar much longer than I've been president. Maybe I can use that to my advantage. I did a good enough job as Mayor of Philadelphia battling bipolar to be elected to Governor of Pennsylvania and, finally, President of the United States.

"Was he experiencing manic symptoms when he was trying to broker peace in the Middle East?" Senator Platner says from his wheelchair on set with Dan Harris at CBS. "I don't know, just like I won't know whether President Pappas will be in the throes of mania or depression whenever he makes key decisions for this country going forward."

I'll have to get on top of this. Collins, I can handle. But Platner? He just lost a son and piling on would look bad. Plus, he has a point.

Why didn't I stick with the gout story? Why the hell didn't I stick with the gout story? This would have blown over quickly, I would have had a better shot at winning a second term and would have been able to make decisions without people questioning my mental health every step along the way.

Ariana and Lin sweep in at that moment, loaded down with shopping bags.

"Your Secret Service detail couldn't have helped you with that?" I ask.

"And have them rummaging through all of this lacy, black lingerie?"

"What did you get, Lin?"

Lin doesn't tell me. She sets her bag down, switches off the TV and wraps me in her arms.

"I'm proud of you, Dad."

I made the right decision. Even if it costs me the presidency.

CHAPTER 50

The first full day of my 25th Amendment cabinet hearings is Doctor Day. We've set aside three days to hear all of the closed-door testimony and Mason has decided to lay out all of his medical evidence on Day One.

"Dr. Feingold," the Secretary of State starts, "will you please enumerate your credentials for the Cabinet members."

"Is this necessary, Shirley?" I ask. "I'll stipulate that Dr. Feingold is an expert on mental health. I'll stipulate that he has the world's largest collection of baseball cards, pre-20th century, if you want."

"Two things," Shirley Harper stares daggers at me. "First, for the purposes of these proceedings, you will address me as Madame Vice President. And, second, this isn't funny."

Dr. Feingold goes on to testify that symptoms of bipolar mania include feeling elated, speaking quickly, feeling self-important and being easily distracted.

"Would you like to cross-examine?" the Vice-President asks when Mason is finished with his direct examination.

"Sorry. I was distracted."

Tarik kicks me under the table.

"Just a couple of questions, Dr. Feingold," I ask. "Would someone who is taking their meds, who is doing everything they are supposed to do to stave off bipolar mania, be in danger of having a manic episode."

"A small chance, but it's possible."

"And those symptoms you enumerated, is it possible anyone in this room who doesn't suffer from bipolar might experience them."

"Again, a small chance, but it's possible."

"Well, the Constitution guaranteed a jury of my peers. Looks like I have one."

Another kick from Tarik, but even Shirley laughs at that one.

Another psychiatrist testifies about the symptoms of depression that plague bipolar sufferers. Another testifies that medication, though very helpful, doesn't guarantee that someone – even someone who has kept his or her bipolar at bay for decades – will never experience a manic or depressive episode again.

"Did you know Teddy Roosevelt won a Nobel Peace Prize, Dr. Kraft?" I ask.

"I am not aware."

"Did you know that Teddy Roosevelt had bipolar?"

"I am aware, but he is an anomaly."

"Yes. An anomaly. A man acknowledged as one of the best presidents we've ever had."

Dr. Kraft has no response.

The day ends, some Cabinet members are more conversant with a disease I've managed to live with for most of my life and I head toward the door. I try to gauge the mood of the various Cabinet members on my way out, but each is wearing his or her best poker face.

"Nice job," my co-counsel and under-the-table kicker, Tarik, says as we walk toward the Oval Office. Tarik didn't ask a single question, but he did a nice job keeping my spirits up when they should have been way, way down.

"We still have a way to go. Want to hoop?"

"Don't you want to prepare for tomorrow?"

"Hooping is preparation. It relaxes me."

CHAPTER 51

Mason starts Day Two by replaying what I call "My Press Conference from Hell," with the help of MIT Chief of Psychiatry Dr. Aaron Levy.

"I've been doing this for a long time – my wife tells me too long," I watch myself saying on screen.

"How would you characterize this statement by President Pappas early in the press conference?" Mason asks Levy.

I'd characterize it as a throwaway line. Hell, I characterize half of what I say in most of my speeches as throwaway lines inserted to keep the audience interested so they stay awake for lines that really matter.

"A little flip," Dr. Levy says. "Possibly a little grandiose. Then again, I don't give speeches."

If you did, Dr. Levy, I'm sure you'd put your audiences to sleep.

Mason clicks to another part of the press conference.

"I've talked about this at length before in impromptu meetings with the press. Weren't you there, Doug? Were you out golfing?"

"And this, Dr. Levy?"

"A little belligerent. Actually, quite belligerent."

You haven't experienced my cross-examination yet, Dr. Levy.

And, finally, Mason clicks to the coup de grace.

"Is golf really a sport, Doug? I mean, you hit a little white ball, you get in a cart and you drive to where that little white ball landed, probably far away from where you intended,

Dougie. Then you hit it again and – I'm guessing in your case, Douglas – hit it about 10 more times before you put it in the hole...."

"And this, Dr. Levy?"

"Again, belligerent. And rambling. And nonsensical."

"All symptoms of full-blown mania?" Mason asks.

"Unfortunately, yes."

I would have stipulated to all of this. I have admitted that I had a manic episode because I didn't take my meds before that press conference.

But Mason wanted to preen and pontificate in front of the rest of the cabinet. I assume he'll be preening and pontificating in front of PNT, DVTV and VOX cameras when this is all over. I've been told that he is on a short list to take my place as the Democratic nominee if I am escorted – maybe in a straitjacket – out of the White House. Mason wasn't about to stipulate and surrender his chance to hog the spotlight.

Mason sits. I stand.

"I only have one question, Dr. Levy?"

"Yes, Mr. President.

"Do you consider golf a sport?"

Laughs all around, except for Mason and Levy.

"I, uh...."

"You don't have to answer that, Dr. Levy. But maybe we can hit the links in the near future. There's a chance I might have a lot of time on my hands."

Levy leaves the room and Mason runs clips of all of my State of the Union addresses. I thought I did well in each but Mason's witness, UC Berkeley Chief of Psychiatry Sandra Eckhardt, points out what she calls "pressured speech" and "loose associations."

And then there are my policy decisions. Mason goes over a number of my more controversial decisions in depth with a few of my critics, closing each examination with, "Do you consider this decision a product of disturbed or illogical thinking?"

The political critics Mason questions predictably agree that each of the decisions was disturbed and illogical, with one of my chief critics saying "It went beyond illogical. It truly was bizarre."

I don't question any of these critics except the last one.

"Did you know, Senator Cranston, that my – your term – *bizarre* decision was approved unanimously in both the House and Senate?"

"I do."

"And that you were one of the Senators who approved?"

"Unfortunately, yes."

"Were you taking your meds that day?"

Chuckles all around – even Shirley, again – before a red-faced Cranston leaves the room.

Tarik, who had been watching Cabinet members intently while I focused on the witnesses, tells me later that Mason scored some points.

But he says I also scored points on cross.

"If you were a betting man...." I start.

"I wouldn't bet. It all depends on what happens when you make your case tomorrow. Have you decided to call any witnesses?"

"Just one. Another doctor."

But not just any doctor. I'm calling Dr. Eric Carty, who knows my state of mind better than anybody. Let's hope he performs as well from the witness box as he does from his psychiatrist's chair.

CHAPTER 52

Eric is easy to spot on the third and final day of the 25th Amendment hearing.

He isn't dressed in full battle regalia, sans helmet, like my Secretary of Defense. He isn't dressed in tailor-made suits like the rest of my cabinet or in a black pants suit like my Vice President. And he isn't sporting a cat-that-swallowed-the-canary grin like Secretary of State Mason, who can't wait to get this little, old hearing out of the way so, I am assuming, he can take my place on the Democratic ticket.

Dr. Carty is wearing a sports jacket, although he eschewed the tie and went with a sweater. And he is sporting the beginnings of a beard. Who does he think he is? Sigmund Freud? I'll talk to him about it the next time I see him in session.

"How long have we been seeing each other, Dr. Carty?" I start.

"Since before you were Mayor of Philadelphia."

"And why did we start seeing each other?"

"You had a manic episode as you were crossing the Walnut Street Bridge. Lucky thing you didn't jump off. You probably thought you could fly."

Dr. Carty goes on to describe our early sessions – *"You were a pain in the ass"* -- our sessions after I was elected Mayor -- *"You were a pain in the ass with a title"* -- and the years we've spent together since I was elected governor and then president.

"And did I have bipolar all that time?"

"Yes."

"And did you ever think my illness interfered with my ability to perform my duties?"

"That one time. I thought you went over the top when you were mayor and tried to turn my office into a parking garage."

Laughs all around, except for Mason. Eric isn't new at this testifying game. He has been called a number of times as an expert witness, in part, because he was first in his class at Harvard and, just as important, because he exudes a folksy charm.

Mason clearly doesn't think Eric is so charming after my longtime psychiatrist goes on to say that my illness is controllable when I take my meds and make my sessions. He even says he might vote for me, "Even though his politics are a little right of mine. Then again, everybody's politics are a little right of mine."

More laughs, interrupted by Mason.

"You're violating doctor-client confidentiality by testifying today, aren't you, Dr. Carty," Mason starts.

"Actually, no. The President gave his permission."

Mason shuffles his papers.

"Is it fair to say that you consider President Pappas a friend?"

"Not really. I always maintain strict boundaries with my clients. As much as I admire the President, I wouldn't socialize with him as long as I was his psychiatrist."

Mason presses on, although that cat-that-swallowed-the-canary grin has vanished.

"And is it fair to say that you would say anything to help your friend?"

"As I said, Secretary Mason, I don't consider President Pappas a friend. Sorry, Mr. President. Maybe at some point in the future when I am not treating you, but not now."

Mason presses Dr. Carty about my press conference flameout, no doubt expecting Eric to push back. Eric doesn't push back.

"It's what happens when someone with bipolar doesn't take his meds," Eric says.

Mason presses Dr. Carty about other speeches, other policy decisions earlier witnesses attributed to my mental illness.

"Oh, I've questioned his mental faculties, too," Eric testifies. "But not because I thought he was having manic episodes. Because people make mistakes. That parking garage decision when he was mayor, I thought he was dead wrong. I've thought he was dead wrong on a number of issues since he was elected president."

Mason shuffles his papers. Eric is proving to be a tougher witness than he expected but Mason is sure he'll find a needle in that haystack of papers to puncture my balloon.

But Mason can't find the needle, so he does something lawyers are taught not to do from Day One in law school: he asks a question when he doesn't know the answer.

"Given that President Pappas is bipolar," Mason starts, "and given, as you've testified, that he has exhibited erratic behavior, do you think President Pappas is fit to hold the office of President of the United States?"

I can almost hear Tarik, who was tops in our law school class, saying 'gotcha.'

Eric milks the scene, tugging on the beard that is barely there and shouldn't be there in the first place.

"More than fit. In fact, I'd vote for him for the first time."

Now, I'm miffed.

"You never voted for me, Dr. Carty?" I ask.

"That parking garage thing. Most things I can forgive, but not that."

CHAPTER 53

I thought Dr. Carty knocked it out of the park. Just the right amount of humor mixed with clinical expertise. I imagine that he kills in front of juries. But this isn't any jury. This is a jury of politicians, some who might want to leap into the Democratic nominee void that would exist if I am kicked out of the White House.

Tarik thought Dr. Carty knocked it out of the park, too.

But VOX – who is leaking to these guys? -- disagrees. At least Trey Collins does. He's with Brolin Murphy the night after the final day of the hearings, concurrently making a case against my mental fitness and the importance of voting for him in November.

"The president's psychiatrist got in a few good lines," Collins says. "But what is he? A standup comedian? And think about what I just said: the president's psychiatrist. Do we need a president who has to consult a psychiatrist to tie his shoes? Will the president's psychiatrist determine whether we continue to back the ridiculous Middle East peace talks? Will the president's psychiatrist be the man behind the scenes determining if we should defund the police, if we should abolish the Second Amendment, if we should open our borders to murderers and rapists from Mexico?"

"But seriously, Trey."

"I am being serious."

DVTV went the other way.

"I have a therapist," Bekka Mornay says. I don't know if that helps me.

"Heck, I'd wager that most of the people on the DVTV staff – my rapping friend, Ari Melman, excepted – have therapists. Don't you want your newspeople to be as mentally fit as possible? And that's what therapy is all about: being in tip-top shape mentally. President Pappas is probably in better mental shape than most of the presidents we've had, especially the one who wanted to divert billions of dollars away from school lunches and build a 40-foot wall around Mexico."

I'm watching TV in the White House living room but can hear Lin cheering from the bedroom.

"You go, girl!"

PNT's Jalen Johnson plays it down the middle. Yes, it looks like President Pappas has a chance to withstand the 25th Amendment challenge. And, yes, it looks like President Pappas will be the Democratic nominee.

"What plays with died-in-the-wool Democrats might not play with Independents in November, though," Johnson says. "And that's the portion of the electorate President Pappas and Senator Collins will be wooing in the general election."

What all of the commentators and all of the politicians think now doesn't matter, though. The only thing that matters is what those 12 people gathered for the 25th Amendment hearing think.

Shirley Harper promised that she would render her decision by the end of the week. If the Cabinet rules against me, it will go to Congress for a vote.

"You have my vote, Dad," Lin says after she and Ariana join me in the living room.

"Me, too, if you wash the dishes tonight," Ariana says.

Love and respect from my wife and daughter should be enough.

But it isn't. We have a lot of work to do in this country. I want to be the one doing it over the next four years.

CHAPTER 54

A week goes by, and I have no answer even though I expected Shirley to drop the 25th Amendment challenge or pass it on to Congress by now.

I do have a win in the Michigan primary, though. But it was the lowest turnout in Michigan in over three decades and Brolin Murphy has been speculating aloud that I'll be replaced on the ticket whether I get past the Pappas-is-crazy challenge or not.

A second week goes by, and I finally hear from Shirley. But it isn't the news I wanted. It isn't the news I didn't want either. It's news that the Cabinet is deadlocked, and she is trying to get a consensus.

I win Illinois but, again, the support for me is tepid. Sixty-two percent of Democrats, in a Pew Research poll, say that they want someone else to head the ticket. I wouldn't be surprised if Paschall is vetting candidates daily to see if somebody – anybody – would be better than me.

"There's always Spector and Walsh," Tarik tells me during an ease-the-tension game of one-on-one a week before Super Tuesday. "You're still president and they already offered a job. I assume you'll take me with you."

"You want to hitch your wagon to a disgraced former president?"

"A job's a job."

Finally, with Super Tuesday a day away, Gladys buzzes me as I sit in my Oval Office going over the infrastructure bill. It took a 25th Amendment challenge and the need to focus on something – anything – to take my mind off the 25th Amendment and get me to focus on a bill that has been sitting on my desk far too long. I'm on Page 251, Part C, Subparagraph A and realize that the legislation isn't too bad.

"It's Vice President Harper," Gladys says. "And a surprise guest."

Shirley walks in, expressionless. I've gotten pretty good at reading people, what with all of the international negotiations I've participated in and all of the bluffs I've seen during four years of White House poker games. But I can't read Shirley.

Maybe I should read something into the fact that she is with Secretary of State Mason, my chief tormentor during the 25th Amendment Cabinet hearings.

"Shirley. James," I say. "Can I get you anything? Coffee? Tea? A new nameplate on the Oval Office door?"

"We won't be staying long," Shirley says.

Uh. Oh.

Shirley sits on the couch. Mason stands behind her. I get a bottle of scotch that has been sitting next to my desk waiting for a unique occasion. Getting drummed out of the presidency certainly is unique. So was the sinking of the Titanic.

"You're staying," Shirley says before I can crack the bottle. "But it wasn't easy."

"No," Mason says. "It was hard as hell."

Shirley goes on to explain that the Cabinet was deadlocked about recommending my ouster to Congress before the Secretary of the Interior changed his mind and decided I should stay.

Mason goes on to say that they wanted unanimity, but it became apparent after one week that some of the Cabinet members, even though they liked me personally, felt that it was their duty under the Constitution to boot me out of the White House.

Phew. I survived. As long as Paschall doesn't decide to go another route, I'll be running against Collins in November.

I offer Shirley a scotch. She's a teetotaler and turns me down.

I offer Mason a glass and he grabs the bottle. Mason has been seen at just about every D.C. watering hole, often in the company of women who wouldn't give him the time of day if he wasn't Secretary of State, and is a two-fisted drinker.

"Sorry for your loss," I say, handing him a glass.

"My loss? I wanted you to win. That performance you saw me give in there, you think a guy who used to go to court for a living could be that bad without trying?"

And I thought he wanted me out so he could head the Democratic ticket.

"Shirley would have been your replacement," James says. "But she turned Paschall down. Shirley loves you. For the life of me, I don't know why."

"And you?"

"I don't love you, but you might lose in November and I'll have a better chance four years from now. No disrespect, Mr. President."

I toast with Mason. And I extend my glass to Shirley, who returns my gesture with a hug.

"Don't listen to James," she says. "You're going to kick Collins's butt. But you better get off yours."

CHAPTER 55

On to Super Tuesday.

I might have won my 25th Amendment battle, but there are 16 states and 1,400 delegates up for grabs today and Patricia Paschall wants results. More specifically, she wants results indicating that the American public won't mind voting for a bipolar president in November.

The only competition I have left on the ballot is Senator Jerry Blavard of Wisconsin. Blavard entered late, spouting a populist message that mirrors Collins. He barely made a dent in his one primary, but polls show him gaining momentum since the 25th Amendment proceedings. Voters will let Paschall know whether he is more viable than me today.

"Blavard might have a shot four years from now," Tarik tells me during a whistle stop in Tennessee. "But not now. A one-term senator who barely squeaked by in his state? The guy has charisma, but you need charisma *and* a track record."

"He doesn't have a track record of mental illness, though. We'll see how that plays today."

I pick off a couple of states early but results from Texas and California, the states with the most delegates, won't come in until later.

"Let's hoop," Tarik says when we return to the White House. "It'll get your mind off something you shouldn't be worried about anyway. The nomination is in the bag. Don't you want to add the cherry on top: beating me in a game of one-on-one?"

"Shut up."

Blavard wins Delaware.

"Delaware's barely there," Tarik says.

He wins Wisconsin.

"What did you expect?" Tarik says. "It's his home state."

But even Tarik's confidence starts to wain when Blavard edges me in Minnesota, a swing state that will be key in November.

"Got to give the guy credit," Tarik says. "But I still don't think he has a chance."

"It doesn't matter what you think. It matters what Patricia Paschall thinks. Blavard does well enough today and she throws all of that Democratic Party money his way. I won as an Independent once. I won't be able to do it twice."

Did I make a mistake announcing that I was bipolar? Is this country ready to accept a guy who could go manic if he forgets to take his meds? The fact that the voters have been led the last four years by a guy who has forgotten to take his meds for a few days doesn't matter. Now, every slip I make will be attributed to my bipolar, not to a guy who makes mistakes just like very president who ever occupied this office.

Early returns from Texas aren't good.

"President Pappas might have won the battle, somehow convincing his Cabinet cronies that he is fit to occupy the White House," Brolin Murphy says. "But it looks like he might lose the war."

"Senator Blavard is a lightweight," Bekka Mornay says. "But he might be a lightweight who is running against Trey Collins in November."

Et tu, Bekka?

"She doesn't know what she's talking about." Lin has been watching election coverage from the bedroom with Ariana. She knows when her father needs moral support.

"I thought you liked her."

"Only when she agrees with you."

And, just like that, the tide turns. I win Utah. I win Oklahoma. I surprisingly take Alabama, where Blavard and his populist message – *"Collins wants to build a 20-foot wall; mine will be 30!"* – was supposed to be a plus.

Lin starts to head back to the bedroom.

"You're not going anywhere, kid," I say, pulling her back to the couch. "You're my good luck charm."

I take the rest of the states, coming from behind in Texas and notching a resounding victory in California. American Samoa only has six electoral votes and I get them. It won't matter much come Democratic Convention time, but maybe Ariana, Lin and I will get a discount on beach umbrellas when we vacation there.

"Are you still going to have time for me when you're ending racism, ensuring world peace and forgiving my student loans over the next four years?" Lin asks.

"I'll always have time for you, but don't be so sure about me forgiving your student loans."

Paschall phones to congratulate me. So does Shuler. Even Trey Collins calls to tell me that I'll be a worthy opponent in November.

"We should keep this election clean, Trey. I won't say anything bad about you and you won't mention my bipolar."

"Fat chance, chief."

I'm riding a high. After all of the 25th Amendment angst, after my Super Tuesday angst and, before that, all of the anxiety I experienced when I was deciding whether to tell the country about my bipolar, I'm one of two people left standing.

But I manage to come down from my high long enough to take my meds before bed. I've learned my lesson. At least, I think I have.

CHAPTER 56

Dr. Carty and I haven't had a therapy session, unless you count him swatting away the Secretary of State during the 25th Amendment hearing, for months.

I want to call his appearance in front of the Cabinet therapy. It certainly made me feel better. But Eric doesn't agree.

"You can't mess around with bipolar," he says, halfway into our post-Super Tuesday session. "One slip, just one, and you're off the wall manic or bordering-on-suicide depressed."

"I know that."

"Do you?"

Eric turns the calendar on his wall back one page, two pages and circles a date before underlining it. He's being dramatic. Dramatic for a reason.

"This is when you saw me last, except when you prepped me for that hearing," he says. "Since then, we've had one synagogue shooting, one 25th Amendment hearing, one Super Tuesday, a few near wars in the Middle East, and no therapy visits."

"I get your point."

Eric gets up from his chair, walks over to his desk, opens a drawer and extracts a coin.

"My most prized possession," he says, smiling at me.

"With what I pay you, I'd think you can do better than that."

"No, I can't."

Eric flips the coin to me. But it's not just any coin. It's gold. An image of a twisted tree is engraved on it. And the number "40" jumps out at you.

"We didn't know each other 40 years ago," Dr. Carty says.

"Not unless you shot hoops at the Y on Broad Street."

"Football was my game. But that was in college. Forty years ago, I wasn't playing football. I wasn't doing much of anything except seeing how many shots I could down before puking. And then, after a good puke, I'd start all over again."

I'm holding Eric's 40-year Alcoholics Anonymous chip. He's told me about his family, about Harvard, about a lot of things, but he never told me he had a drinking problem. Until now.

"As proud as I am of the work you and I do, as happy as I am being a father to two wonderful daughters and -- from what Jeanne tells me – a good husband, I'm most proud of that little thing you have in your hand."

"You could have told me."

"You would have run out of my Philly office and found another psychiatrist if I told you the first time we met."

He's right.

"Four decades sober," Eric smiles. "Time was, I couldn't make it through four hours without taking another drink."

"Why are you telling me now?"

Eric takes the chip, opens his window and tosses it onto the lawn.

"What are you doing?!"

"I'm telling you now because that chip – my most prized possession – doesn't mean shit if I get too full of myself and throw away my sobriety. Hell, I could tell myself that I must be pretty damn good to be the president's psychiatrist. After telling myself that I'm pretty damn good – better than that; the greatest psychiatrist since Sigmund Freud – I decide to celebrate my greatness with a beer down at McGlinchey's up the road. But it wouldn't end with one beer. There'd be another and another, eventually turning into straight whiskey, and I'd be right back where I started forty years ago."

I shouldn't be stunned, but I am. I'm President of the United States and have the type of mental health disorder that led to my Uncle Tony – well before psychiatry knew what to do with bipolar – spending the last 20 years of his life locked in a mental institution.

Just because Dr. Carty has risen to the top of his profession doesn't mean he has a skeleton-free closet. It doesn't make me feel less of him. In fact, it enhances my respect and I feel honored that he confided in me.

"Don't think you're so great that you can't lose it all, Evan. Don't think you can stop taking your meds, that you can stop seeing me, that you can stop meditating and exercising, especially with all the stressful shit you have coming down the pike. There would be serious repercussions, and not just for you. For your family. For the country."

"I'll see you every week, even if I'm in Jerusalem and am about to sign a peace treaty. I'll do a Zoom session first."

"Sign the treaty first. Anything else, get me on the line."

Our time is up and I'm about to walk out. But I turn, walk back to Eric and hug him. He's my psychiatrist. And, despite what he said at the 25th Amendment hearing, he is a friend. A very good friend.

"One thing I can't understand," I say. "That 40-year chip was your most prized possession. Why did you throw it away?"

"It's a knockoff. The real one's still in my desk. What you saw was for dramatic effect."

CHAPTER 57

The cultural exchange between Israel and Palestine seemed to be going well. Israeli teachers, according to the CIA and the U.S. Embassy in Jerusalem, had been greeted with relatively open arms in Gaza. And Palestinian teachers, according to the same agencies, had overflow enrollment in their Tel Aviv classrooms.

"I truly am shocked," Noah told me last week via conference call. "Maybe it was time. Maybe my people and Farid's people have tired of all the bloodshed."

"Prime Minister Noah will be visiting my home in Gaza City in the very near future," Farid said during the same conference call. "This truly is historic."

Or wishful thinking.

Islamic Jihad and their leadership have been critical of Farid since the peace talks started. IJ has called Farid "an infidel" and "a traitor" and an "anathema to all Palestinians who long for a homeland free of the Zionists."

And that's the nice part.

A bomb exploded at Farid's mosque two weeks ago. Farid would have been at the mosque, but one of his wives gave birth to Farid's fifth child that day and Farid was at her side. Twenty-three worshippers at the mosque weren't so fortunate. They died along with a suicide bomber with links to Islamic Jihad.

"I will take care of this," Farid said when I asked if he wanted the U.S.

to intervene.

An IJ leader's body was found, riddled with bullets, the next day. Whether Farid had anything to do with it, I don't know. I probably should ask Farid, but I don't want to know. It is an internal matter and I do not want to do anything to jeopardize what has been a tenuous peace.

Noah has met with strong resistance from the ultra-conservative Likud faction of the Israeli Parliament. "We will not be driven to the sea," Likud leader Lev Sonenshein said. "And, make no mistake, that is what the Palestinians want. These peace talks, they are merely something the terrorists can hide behind while they plot the next attack on our people."

"I'll handle this," Noah, much like Farid before him, told me when I offered to help. "My opponents in the Knesset, they are worried more about getting reelected than keeping the peace."

Sonenshein was censured during an emergency session of the Knesset the following week. It didn't stop him from talking – "*The Prime Minister seems to care more about Palestinians than he does Israelis*" -- but polls show that Israelis are firmly behind the peace talks and the relative peace that has existed since they began.

Rachel, the first woman Tarik has allowed to get beyond the fifth date in over 20 years, isn't so optimistic.

Ariana and I invited Tarik and Rachel to the White House for a post-Super Tuesday celebration that included lobster salad, one of the best Israeli dishes I ever had – Tarik better hold onto this woman – and a screening of a movie by a hot, new Hollywood director who won't remain so hot if he doesn't include more action and less idyllic, pastoral scenes in his films.

The night went well for the most part.

Tarik held the Israeli diplomat's hand for 14 straight minutes – I've timed these things since our bachelor days – and we even got Ariana to play Scrabble with us to close the night. Ariana and I won, which should make

Ariana feel better about Scrabble. But I overruled Ariana on a move late in the game, which probably will lead to me playing alone against the computer yet again.

Rachel, who makes periodic visits to Israel to visit her family, made a troubling statement, though, as Tarik was about to escort her home. It seemed like she was holding something in all night, but I attributed it to normal boyfriend-girlfriend problems.

"The peace talks are a noble experiment," she said just before she left. "But they will not work in the long run. And peace with Palestine isn't the end of it. Everybody, led by Iran, is against my country."

Rachel might be right for Tarik. I sincerely hope so because my lifelong friend needs a good woman to make him truly happy.

But I hope she is wrong about the talks. Peace in the Middle East would be my biggest accomplishment in nearly four years as president. If things don't work out in the Middle East, it could be what takes me down in November.

CHAPTER 58

Tarik and I had a Plan B whenever we were bogged down studying torts or contracts or constitutional law at Temple, not knowing – and, sometimes, not caring – whether we'd pass our bar exams, become lawyers and have to slave away the rest of our lives writing contracts nobody could understand or arguing for criminal defendants we couldn't stand.

Plan B was simple. We'd rent the cheapest shack we could find on a Caribbean Island – Tarik wanted Jamaica; I wanted St. Croix – set up shop on the beach and get vacationers to pay us for answering sports questions.

"You take hockey," Tarik would say.

"Because it's a mostly White sport?"

"Yep. You think someone would believe a Black man telling them Gordie Howe made 23 all-star teams?"

"Who's Gordie Howe?"

"Doesn't matter. You're White. Make things up as you go along. They'll believe you."

Instead, I sat in the Oval Office last week, four months before the Democratic Convention in my hometown of Philadelphia, and put the finishing touches on an infrastructure bill that has been the bane of my existence for far too long.

Shockingly, the networks are unanimous praising a bill that has no chance getting past the House but has every chance of getting me brownie points going into the general election.

"People don't talk about infrastructure because they don't understand infrastructure," Ari Melman said. "But I'm an infrastructure guy from a ways back and, let me tell you, President Pappas knocked this one out of the park like Biggie and Tupac knocked their competition out of the park."

New and improved gun control legislation also is on my agenda. There already have been more mass shootings this year than the last two years combined, and Republicans and Democrats alike know things have to change.

How things change is another matter. Republicans want more guns so the common man can protect himself. Democrats – and I'm one of them now – want less assault rifles and more mental health interventions. The NRA wants to make money, which probably will hold up the passage of meaningful gun legislation for years.

Still, Congress sent me a gun control bill two weeks ago which I am considering signing. It doesn't give the Democrats everything we want. It doesn't give the Republicans everything they want. But it's a hell of a lot better than what we have in place now.

"I agree with President Pappas about the mental health checks," Collins says during what has turned into a weekly sit-down with Brolin Murphy. "Too bad we didn't have mental health checks on presidential candidates when he was running."

I can't wait to get Collins on a debate stage in the fall. Yes, he's younger, something Ariana reminds me about whenever we watch him on TV. And, yes, he is charismatic. Ariana also reminds me of this, although she says I am charismatic, too. But she only said it after I promised that her parents could join us on a week-long vacation to Hawaii after I get elected.

Collins doesn't know what the hell he's talking about when it comes to mental illness, though. I do. Hell, I've been living with this for much of my life. Collins will come across as a bully on a debate stage, I'll come across as the enlightened one and will roll to my second term in the White House.

"You might be enlightened," Tarik tells me whenever I broach the subject, "but I'm not so sure about the country. I'd focus on something else in the debates."

"I'm the President. I can focus on whatever I want."

"You'll be an ex-president who can focus on his next job."

Which could be Plan B, getting paid to answer sports questions on an island in the Caribbean.

I better bone up on hockey.

CHAPTER 59

I'm not a big horror movie fan, but I managed to make it through one that lasted three days and left me hiding under the White House covers.

The Republican National Convention in July starred Trey Collins, included assorted bit players and focused on what a great guy Collins is and what a bad guy I am. It had it all. The ominous music. Chants of "Lock Him Up," although I still don't know what crime I committed, and a rousing closing from Collins.

"Do we want four more years of misery?" Collins asked after the longest rendition of the National Anthem I ever heard. "Four more years of a tanking economy? Four more years of crime-ridden cities? Four more years of a leader with a terrible border policy, assuming that he actually looks at a map and knows there is a border?"

Ariana and I are sitting in bed, watching this bright, shiny, 65-inch TV delivered to me as a present from outgoing Senator Johnston.

"I know there's a border."

"I'm sure you do, honey."

"Canada to the North, Mexico to the South and what's to the West?"

"The Pacific Ocean. Want some chips?"

Collins hammers on what he considers my "pie-in-the-sky" Middle East policy.

"Maybe President Pappas, in his last days in office, can focus more on problems we can fix in this country than problems he can't fix in other countries."

Collins hammers on practically all of my other policies, including ones he and I agree on.

"Restore law and order," Collins said. "Restore power to the people, not to a big government that wants to take power from the people. Restore sanity to this country."

Ariana hands me a chip.

"Sanity? That was a direct shot at me."

"Not so direct. A metaphorical shot, maybe. But not a direct shot. Anyway, you'll have your chance next week."

Collins's attacks on me are no surprise. It's what party nominees have done since the writers of the Constitution ensured when they created the First Amendment and free speech. Republicans and Democrats alike can say whatever they want about each other and get away with it, fact-checkers be damned.

It's what Collins did to end the convention that came as a surprise. My rival for the Presidency has been teasing for months about who he would nominate as a running mate. Would it be a woman to counter my running mate? Would it be an African American to pick off Black votes Democrats have been getting forever?

In the end, though, Collins chooses a White man. But not any White man. He picks Morris Platner, whose son was murdered in the synagogue shooting. It's a smart move. Not only will Collins come after my Middle East policy. He'll come after it with a man who lost his son at the hands of a terrorist.

"How do I compete with that?" I ask Tarik later.

"You don't. You sympathize and you utilize every chance you get to tell the American public why peace in the Middle East is beneficial to everybody, especially Americans."

The Democratic Convention in August is everything the Republican Convention wasn't. Sweetness. Light. Good music. Republican President Ronald Regan referred to America as the "shining city on the hill." I am almost blinded by the sweetness and light emanating from my 65-inch TV screen.

"The critics on Rotten Tomatoes would pan this," I say. "Too syrupy. Too sweet. No nuance."

"But the audience score would be through the roof," Ariana says. "People aren't looking for nuance. They want to feel good."

I finally take the stage at the Wells Fargo Center in Philadelphia to deliver my acceptance speech. This is after a few days touring my hometown with Tarik, gobbling up every free cheesesteak South Philly had to offer.

Like Collins, I talk about the economy. In my speech, though, it is thriving. Like Collins, I talk about law and order. In my speech, though, I point to a crime rate that is down 11 percent nationally. Like Collins, I talk immigration. But I focus on all the contributions immigrants – I include my grandparents, who immigrated from Greece – have contributed to this country.

Confetti falls from the ceiling. Tons and tons of confetti. Thank God, I'm not a member of the cleanup crew. The crowd cheers, Lin hugs me, Ariana kisses me and various relatives – some of whom I haven't seen for years – smile and wave to the crowd.

It is my first convention. When you run as an Independent like I did last time, you sit in your living room, broadcast to millions of people watching on various social media platforms and hope there are a lot of smiling face emojis from #SchenectadySally when she critiques your speech.

I am a walking smiley face emoji as I leave the stage and head to the airport to be whisked back to Washington on Air Force One.

The smile lasts until the next day.

That is when I hear of yet another terrorist bombing in Israel, this one in Haifa.

CHAPTER 60

Noah insisted at first that I come alone, although he finally agreed that I could bring Tarik. I wanted to call Farid and have him tour the wreckage in Haifa with us, but Noah nixed that idea.

"I know you want this to work," Noah said. "So, do I. But at this point, I don't know if I can trust any Palestinian, Farid included."

Air Force One lands in Haifa the day after the Democratic Convention. Tarik has accompanied me, but I haven't alerted any members of the media. This isn't a photo op. This is serious and the peace talks hang in the balance.

From scenes on TV and from intelligence reports that have been sent to me, I expected, at most, half a Haifa city block laying in ruins. Unfortunately, four city blocks have been leveled. This isn't the work of a suicide bomber. It is the result of rockets launched from Gaza City, Noah tells me, rockets – the Mossad has told Noah – that might have been launched at Farid's behest.

"Three-hundred, seventy-two dead," Noah says as we walk in what used to be a thriving open-air market. "Over 800 wounded. Mark my words, there will be retribution. There will be blood."

"But..."

"No buts. My people have suffered in silence long enough. It's time to end that silence."

"Even if it means the end of the peace?"

"Look around you. Does this look like peace?"

It doesn't. Whatever goodwill the peace talks fostered, that goodwill probably will end. A couple of well-placed bombs, over a thousand dead and wounded Israelis and yet another war in an endless cycle of wars is about to continue.

But who did this? Was it Farid? I tell myself it wasn't, but maybe that is because I want so badly for the peace talks to work, and Farid was poised to sign off on what I consider one of the most important treaties of the last two centuries. Farid called to tell me he had nothing to do with it. I took his call on Air Force One as we jetted to Haifa, but I didn't tell him where we were going.

Was it one of the many factions in Palestine that want the peace talks to fail? Farid has been a pariah in his native land since teaming with Noah to make the peace and his foes – particularly Islamic Jihad – would like to see him fall flat on his face.

Was it one of Noah's many rivals within the Knesset? Twitter-world is on fire with speculation that Israelis manufactured this catastrophe in hopes of ending the peace and giving Israel carte blanche to attack Palestine. I don't believe most of what I read on social media and I don't believe this. Still, American universities – including a few Ivy League institutions – are planning another wave of anti-Israel, pro-Palestine demonstrations.

"It used to pay getting an Ivy League education," Tarik says after we return to our hotel room. "Seems like kids come out dumber after they go to those places."

"But they'll still make more money than your average Temple grad."

"Except you and me."

"Including you and me."

Tarik and I dine on our balcony at the foot of Mount Carmel looking out at the Port of Haifa. I didn't want anything special, and probably made my hosts do more work than necessary trying to scrounge around for a couple of hamburgers.

Tarik tells me that he spoke to Rachel before he left, and she wasn't surprised by the bombing.

"I hope you told her to keep our trip to herself," I say.

"Fat chance of that. She's an Israeli spy."

"Seriously?"

"No, not seriously. You want serious? I think I'm falling in love. After the election, I plan to ask her to marry me."

This is the best news I have gotten in a long, long time. Hopefully, though, it won't cut down on the basketball or poker time I spend with my life-long best friend.

We finish our dinner in silence. Tarik tried to lighten the mood – *The Phillies won last night!* -- but I can't get what I saw out of my head, and we eat in silence.

"What will you do?" Tarik finally asks.

"Try to salvage the peace."

"And how will you do that?"

"I have absolutely no idea."

CHAPTER 61

Noah and I meet one more time before Tarik and I fly back to the States. The Israeli Prime Minister books the ironically named Shalom Restaurant for the night, surrounds it with armed guards and orders for the table.

"This could be our last meal together for the foreseeable future," Noah says. "Please enjoy yourselves."

But I can't. Noah's personal chef has cooked a number of gourmet Israeli dishes, the chef at the best American restaurant in Haifa has made a decidedly un-American dish, coq au vin, and there is enough wine to keep Noah, his right-hand man, Schlomo Glickstein, Tarik and I drunk for weeks.

But I don't feel like drinking. I don't feel like eating much, either, even the coq au vin.

I want to give life to all of those killed in Haifa. I want to breathe life into peace talks that are failing. Most of all, I want to erase the memory of that hand – a small child's hand, damn it – I saw partially obscured by a rock when I walked through the Haifa rubble.

"Will you at least listen to Farid?" I ask Noah. "He insists that he was not behind the bombing."

"No, I will not listen to Farid. Does it matter? The bombs came from Palestine. Whether he was behind the bombing, whether Islamic Jihad was behind the bombing or whether it was one of a hundred other splinter groups that want to wipe my country from the face of the Earth, it doesn't matter."

"Will you listen to me?"

"With all due respect, Mr. President, I do not tell you how to run your country. Please do not tell me how to run mine. You have a good heart. So did the hundreds of Israelis who died in the bombing. They shall have their revenge."

Halfway over the Atlantic Ocean on our way home, I have had a few drinks. As has Tarik. Noah insisted that we take two bottles of wine from the world-renowned Tzora Vineyards, and I obliged. It was an act of good faith. Plus, I want to get blackout drunk. Maybe that will make me forget that child's hand.

Meanwhile, my opponents – and even some people I considered allies – are making political hay at home with something that doesn't feel political right now.

Collins trailed me in the polls two days ago but is up five percentage points now, and is railing on with Brolin Murphy.

"One of the signs of mania is a grandiose sense of self," Collins said. "President Pappas' grandiose sense of self led him to go where so many other presidents before him had gone...and failed. He tried to forge a peace between Israelis and a people who are sworn to obliterate Israel. He failed. And, today, hundreds of people lie dead in Haifa's streets."

DVTV: "Why didn't President Pappas tell the press that he was making an unscheduled trip to Israel to meet with the Israeli Prime Minister?" Bekka Mornay asks. "I'll tell you why. He didn't want the press to see the carnage. He didn't want the press to ask questions that need to be asked. But President Pappas can only hide for so long. And the images of the destruction in Haifa, well, we don't need President Pappas' permission to show them."

Mornay runs pictures of flattened buildings, crying family members and wounded Israelis being hustled into ambulances. I wish there was enough fuel on this plane to pass over America and take me to some secluded island.

Maybe Tarik and I can start Plan B now.

PNT's Jack Tanner is the only one I see on TV who isn't willing to throw me under the bus. He talks about the need for peace. He talks about his Jewish heritage and people in his family who died in the Holocaust, who died in various wars since Israel gained independence in 1948.

"At least, President Pappas tried," Tanner concludes.

Tarik pours what is left of the bottle of wine and extends his glass for a toast.

"Here's to trying," he says. "It's all you can do."

I withhold my toast.

"Fuck that. Get my Secretary of State on the phone and tell him to meet me at the airport. I'll do more than try."

CHAPTER 62

Secretary of State Mason, who argued against me in the 25th Amendment hearings, is waiting at Andrews Air Force Base. My enemy two weeks ago is one of the people I'll need most if I want to salvage what is left of peace talks.

But he isn't the only one waiting. Vice President Harper, Admiral Nimitz, and other members of the Joint Chiefs of Staff also are waiting.

"What?" I say after I step on the tarmac. "I didn't know you all missed me so much."

"We didn't miss you so much," Nimitz says. "But we had to see you immediately because of what just happened in Palestine."

I assume he's talking about the Haifa bombing. I'm only partially right.

In the time it took for us to switch off all communication devices on Air Force One as we started our decent to Andrews, Israel struck back. And Noah, true to his word, struck back hard to exact revenge for all of those killed in Haifa.

Gaza City was one of the targets. Nimitz tells me that Noah was going after the tunnels Islamic Jihad uses for escape routes. Unfortunately, Islamic Jihad chose to build those tunnels under schools and hospitals. Patients at the hospitals and students at the schools have been part of the collateral damage.

"Collateral damage?" I say to Nimitz. "It's damage. Period."

Noah, who clearly was prepared for the moment when the tenuous peace was shattered, also unleashed drone strikes that took out Islamic Jihad's Abu Rasir, Sons of Jihad leader Nasir Nadal and River to the Sea head Ibrahim Fatwal.

There was little to no collateral damage in those strikes and, after a thorough briefing by Nimitz, Mason and my Vice President on our ride back to the White House, I wonder if Noah should have started with the more targeted strikes and left the collateral damage strikes until later.

"He wanted to send a message," Mason says. "You slaughter 1,000 Israelis, we kill 2,000 Palestinians. A few terrorist leaders weren't enough."

Farid, thus far, has not been a target of Noah's wrath. He is holed up underground in Rafah, although attempts to reach him have proven fruitless. I am guessing that he might be the next target of Islamic terrorist organizations who chafed at a possible peace with Israel.

"We need to reach him," I say. "And we need to contact Noah. Farid, Noah and I are the ones brokering the peace."

"Brokering? Don't you mean 'broke?'" Nimitz says.

"I have a few cards to play," I say. "Humpty Dumpty might be broken, but let's see if we can put him back together again."

The best part of the day – the only good part of the day – is when I walk in the front door of the White House. Actually, it's me and my Secret Service contingent walking in the front door, which detracts from the feel-good moment of Ariana, also surrounded by her Secret Service contingent, rushing into my arms.

"Are you okay?" she says.

"Better than I was a minute ago. Where's Lin?"

On cue, Lin rushes in from the bedroom.

Our little family tableau must look like countless other happy family scenes playing out across the country. Spouse returns from work. Other spouse greets him or her lovingly. Daughter pulls herself away from the TV long enough to greet returning parent with a hug. And then husband, wife and daughter sit down to meatloaf and mashed potatoes for dinner.

But Ariana, Lin and I won't have meatloaf and mashed potatoes tonight. The White House chef has prepared duck a l'orange, and I can't wait to get to it after a long day of meetings and little food.

Our little Hallmark moment differs from other Hallmark moments in one other respect: the fate of the world depends on what happens sometime after we eat.

CHAPTER 63

The Joint Chiefs of Staff beat the civilians to the Situation Room. I guess that's why they're Joint Chiefs and the rest of us aren't.

There's Admiral Nimitz, Chairman of the Joint Chiefs, dressed in what looks like full battle regalia. There's Vice Chairman Marshall Grady, dressed like he's ready for battle, too, although his shirt is untucked. There's Chief of Staff and Army General Randall A. Heathrow and Commandant of the Marine Corps, Joseph Conrad.

I'm intimidated. I'm their boss and I'm intimidated. I guess that's what all the battle regalia is about.

"Who ordered out for pizza?" I start. No one cracks a smile, even the civilian contingent I brought with me: Tarik, Vice President Harper and Secretary of State Mason.

Nimitz clicks to an overhead map of the Middle East and zooms in on Qatar.

"This," Nimitz says, "is our largest base in the Middle East. Those Palestinian bastards want to bomb Israel again, we'll be ready."

"For now," I say, "the Israelis seem to be handling the bombing thing on their own."

Grady takes the remote from Nimitz and zooms in on Bahrain. And Kuwait. And Saudi Arabia. And the United Arab Emirates.

"If it's war these terrorists want, they came looking in the wrong place," Grady says. "We got bases all over the place. Palestine will be a parking lot by the time we get through with it. Hell, those other countries could be parking lots, too."

"Again, General Grady, Israel is handling things so far. And it's not war I want. It's peace."

I get it. The men sitting in front of me have been trained for war and all of them have fought in conflicts around the globe. It's what they do best and, judging by what I've heard so far, it's what they want to do best in the near future.

"How, exactly, do you want to come to a peaceful resolution?" General Heathrow asks.

This is why I brought Mason and my Vice President along. Tarik is here strictly for moral support. He knows a lot about winning elections. He has no experience – other than his budding relationship with an Israeli diplomat – in the Middle East.

Mason emphasizes, as we discussed before this meeting, that everything is preliminary. How we act depends on how Israel acts. How we respond depends on how the Palestinians respond.

My Secretary of State starts by telling the Joint Chiefs that Israel has been America's strongest ally for decades and that the U.S. does not want to jeopardize a relationship with our only true partner in the Middle East.

He goes on to explain that there are other players in what is unfolding – Iran, chief among them – and that economic sanctions and/or military force might be necessary in the future.

"My hope," Mason says, "is that this retaliation by Israel is the last retaliation. My hope is that we can get back to business as usual – or as close to business as usual – after the dust settles."

Conrad laughs.

"The dust ain't settling," Conrad says, "until we turn that place into dust. Hell, it's already sand. We don't have far to go."

Shirley has been sitting back listening. She did a stint in the Army before getting into politics, but never served overseas. Her father rose to the level of captain in the Navy.

The Vice President has a healthy respect for our armed services. But she has an even healthier respect for peace.

"As of two weeks ago," Shirley says, "the peace process was working. As of two weeks ago, Palestine and Israel were enjoying their longest sustained period of peace since the Oslo Accords."

Conrad laughs again.

"Little lady," he says, "that treaty, or whatever you want to call it, ain't worth the paper it'll be printed on."

It's hard to tell when Shirley is mad. She's gotten angry at me a number of times, but I usually don't realize it until later after she took time to calm down, organize her thoughts and dash off a letter that is both respectful and leaves me bloodied and bowed.

She is angry now. And she doesn't have time to dash off a respectful letter to Commandant Conrad.

"This little lady," Shirley says, "outranks you. You want to sit in on these meetings again, Commandant, I suggest you address me as Madame Vice President."

Conrad isn't laughing anymore.

"But the President, the Secretary of State, me and everybody in the Cabinet wants peace," Shirley continues. "At the same time, we want the Joint Chiefs to continually update us on our military options while we explore economic and humanitarian sanctions."

The meeting ends. The Joint Chiefs leave. I'm guessing they'll be cursing Shirley later.

"Well, that was fun," Shirley tells me in the Oval Office later.

"Yes, little lady, it certainly was.

Shirley smiles. I expect a tactfully scathing letter later.

195

CHAPTER 64

I turn on the TV the next day and expect to see Brolin Murphy railing against me, Trey Collins railing against me and commentators on DVTV and PNT using more nuance as they rail against me.

I get what I expected.

Collins: "Day One after I'm elected, I'll fix this." Yeah, right, Trey. Just like all of my predecessors brought peace to the Middle East.

Melman: "You pick your fights. Maybe President Pappas picked the wrong one."

Tanner: "The President, my sources tell me, is investigating a myriad of solutions. Let's hope one of the peaceful solutions triumphs over alternatives that result in more Israeli deaths, more Palestinian deaths and, possibly, World War III."

And then a scroll across the bottom of the TV interrupts Tanner:

Breaking News: Mass shooting in Texas high school.

I would prefer a day of commentators taking me to task for my policies in the Middle East. Instead, the country has to deal with yet another mass shooting and a mass shooting death toll this year that eclipses the death toll thus far in the Middle East.

The numbers from the latest shooting at a high school in Parkview Texas, are chilling.

211.

The number of lives lost when a gunman broke into an auditorium and opened up with an AK-47 assault rifle.

88.

The number of students and teachers injured, most of whom were transported to the local hospital.

4.

The number of teachers who won't be teaching anymore. Aida Sterling, Seve Vamara, Juan Camara and Julie Smythe were conducting an assembly on, of all things, gun safety when the gunman broke in. Vamara and Smythe, I learn, died with their bodies draped over students. The students lived. Vamara and Smythe didn't. They are the true heroes and I'll go through the usual – *usual, damn it, usual* -- awarding of posthumous medals sometime this week.

Why? *Why?!* I didn't expect to get any answers when I boarded Air Force One for Parkview an hour later and don't expect to get them now that I am at the high school meeting with parents and teachers and police. But I want to feel the pain, knowing that my pain can't come close to the pain of the parents who won't see their children again. This is personal and I want it to sound very personal every time I make a speech about guns and deaths and a Second Amendment that has been twisted like a pretzel so politicians, lobbyists and the gun industry can keep churning out profits.

"Thank you for coming, Mr. President," the principal, Juana Juarez, tells me when I enter the school flanked by my Secret Service contingent. "It will mean a lot to the parents."

Juarez is thanking me for coming. But I'll go back to Washington. Ms. Juarez will be here long after I leave to start conducting something that seems so meaningless right now: my campaign.

Juana has assembled a number of parents in the gym. I don't want this to look like another photo op and ask Ms. Juarez to lock the gym door to keep the press out. I want to meet and talk to the parents alone to offer my condolences, to promise that I will do better, that Congress will do better, on gun laws that will make children safer.

Maria Lupo, who lost her daughter, Christina, hugs me.

"It's my fault!" she says through the tears. "It's my fault! Christina said she was sick. I made her go to school to take that test."

George Vasquez wipes away his tears and shakes my hand.

"My son, Diego, was my life."

Maria, George and all of the parents I meet had their lives ripped away from them. You feel their pain when you watch them cry on TV, but you *really* feel their pain when you hug them and say a few words that might help a little as they try to put their lives back together.

That's why I am here. I want to feel their pain. I want this to be even more personal than it was before a 19-year-old former student somehow got past security armed with an assault rifle, set a record for casualties in a school shooting, and then took his own life.

First up when I get back to Washington: I will convene a joint session of Congress to strengthen a barely-there gun proposal that sits on my desk unsigned.

The next thing I'll do when I get back to Washington: I'll go on national television – *again, damn it, again* – and rail against the gun lobbies, the gun makers and the legislators whose inaction allows things like this to happen.

The first thing I find out when I turn on the TV after I fly back to Washington: the gunman who ruined so many lives was bipolar. Hopefully, my announcement that I am bipolar doesn't make this more difficult than it is already.

CHAPTER 65

*O*ur thoughts and prayers go out to the families..."

"*Our thoughts and prayers go out to the families...*"

"*Our thoughts and prayers go out to the families...*"

Pick a senator, any senator, and that's what I am hearing on the news one day after the Parkview massacre. It's what I heard after the last shooting and the shooting before that.

I want all of this self-serving blather to sicken me today. But it doesn't. I feel numb because I have heard it so many times before.

"Just be careful what you say on TV tonight," Tarik warns me when we meet in the Oval Office to discuss my hastily assembled nationally televised Parkview speech. "You have an election to win, and nothing gets accomplished if you aren't in the White House for a second term."

"A lot of good me being in the White House did those kids in Parkview."

Maybe Tarik is right. If Collins is President, there will be a lot more guns, less stringent gun-purchasing laws and more Parkviews.

Britain used to have more mass shootings. They tightened their gun laws and the number of mass shootings plummeted. Same with Australia, New Zealand and Norway. But I don't have to go overseas to find data to support what I know. States in the U.S. that have the loosest gun laws have the most mass shootings.

I might be literally crazy according to Dr. Carty and his psychiatric bible, the DSM-7, but this country's stance on guns takes craziness to another level.

Of course, Collins goes with the same, old NRA song and dance when he speaks to the American public on VOX.

"First, my thoughts and prayers...." Collins starts. I use the time he talks to let us know how much he cares — how much he *really, really cares* — to take a bathroom break.

Back to Collins.

"But guns don't kill people. People kill people," Collins continues. I take the time to pour myself a drink, a stiff drink, and it's not even noon.

And he's still talking when I return to the TV.

"We need a serious person in the White House to deal with this issue," Collins says. Serious? Is he dropping out and ceding the Presidency to me? "President Pappas is not the type of person who can solve this problem...."

Type of person?

"In fact, President Pappas has a mental illness, the same mental illness as the gunman responsible for the Parkview slaughter, and my thoughts and prayers go out to him as he battles this illness...."

Oh, that type of person. And more "thoughts and prayers."

"President Pappas' mental illness prevents him from even buying a gun in some states. Can we really trust a person who can't buy a gun to solve the gun problem? The answer, clearly, is no. And you'll be able to give your answer in November when you elect me as your next President."

I'm not sickened. Collins is a political animal, and he just did what political animals do: he stalked his prey — me — and tried to rip my heart out.

My heart is still beating, although it's beating faster than it was when Collins started talking.

I have a national TV appearance scheduled for tonight. This campaign just got very, very interesting, although I wish it hadn't gotten interesting at the expense of all of those victims Collins is thinking and praying about.

CHAPTER 66

You're going to do what on TV tonight?" Dr. Carty asks.

"Kick Collins' ass. That guy won't be able to show his face in his state, which had more school shootings than any state in the country last year."

"And you actually want to be President?"

"Damn right, I do."

I'm in Eric's office hours before my TV appearance. I want to make sure I eviscerate Collins in front of millions of people for the right reasons. And I want to let off a little steam. Eric has taught me that nothing good ever comes out of making statements in anger, that anger always dissipates and that saying things with a clear head always is the best way to go.

Fuck that. I'm pissed off and want the country to be pissed off, too. And not just at Collins. At all of the people who worship at the altar of the NRA before going to an altar in their local church on Sundays to say prayers for the victims of gun violence.

"Speaking of death, you have a death wish," Eric says. "You don't want to be president."

"All of that campaigning I did to win the Democratic nomination was just for fun?"

"Or ego. You still haven't won anything. And the guy you dislike most, the guy you plan to blast tonight, will be the one preventing meaningful gun legislation if you lose."

Dr. Carty might be right. The best political move, the one I probably need to make to win those swing states, might be to give a politically correct speech that will appease the anti-gun people while not turning off Second Amendment folks who might vote for me in November.

But those parents I met yesterday in Texas aren't thinking about politics today. They are looking at the empty spots at the dinner table that used to be occupied by their children.

"And if I win? If I get another four years in the White House and don't accomplish anything, Eric?"

"You'll accomplish plenty."

"Ulysses S. Grant."

"What?

I tell Eric that Grant was a great Civil War general generally considered one of the weakest, most ineffective presidents in U.S. history.

"He served two terms," I say. "I'd rather serve one term if it means actually doing something."

"And you think you'll actually accomplish something if you go fire and brimstone on national TV tonight?'

"I haven't decided what I'll do yet. You tell me I shouldn't say anything out of anger. But you also tell me to be true to myself, and my true self is pissed as hell."

CHAPTER 67

Photos of the four teachers murdered in Parkview sit on the Oval Office desk for my national TV address. There isn't space for photos of the 211 children killed or they would be up here, too. But I'll get to the children.

Everything else is pretty much the same for one of my national TV appearances. The American flag behind me. The white shirt, blue suit and red tie. A teleprompter which will scroll down the speech Jim Banoff wrote for me today.

"And stick to it the script this time," Tarik tells me before the lights go on and the cameras start rolling. "You don't want to piss voters off. It's a damn good speech."

I'm sure it is. Jim Banoff is a damn good writer. I hope he doesn't quit after I give my talk.

"Good evening, America," I start. "But yesterday wasn't such a good day for the four teachers you see before me, gunned down in a senseless school shooting in Parkview, Texas, for all of the 211 killed, for the 88 injured, for all of their family members and friends, and for all of the teachers and students murdered in so many other senseless school shootings that have put a stain on that American flag you see behind me tonight.

"Unfortunately, it has turned into an all-too-typical day. Americans wake up, turn on the news and are greeted by a newscaster, in an appropriately solemn voice, intoning that someone, somehow, entered a school, a church, an office and took out an assault rifle to commit murder. And then you hear all of the senators and congressmen offering up thoughts and prayers for the dead, some even promising that things will change."

I haven't strayed from Jim Banoff's script yet. Hell, he's making me sound good.

"But things never seem to change, do they? We allow ourselves a few days to mourn and then Washington goes on with business as usual. The occasional gun safety bill passes the House and maybe even makes it through the Senate, but the bills that reach my desk always are window dressing. Guns keep finding their way into the hands of people who should not own them. People find their way into classrooms when they should have been stopped at the door. And, at the end of the day, you have countless students dead. In the Parkview case, countless students dead and the lives of the four heroes you see on my desk snuffed out."

I pick up the photo of Juan Camara and tell America that he was the first person in his family to graduate from college and had been voted best teacher at Parkview five years running. I pick up the photo of Aida Sterling and talk about how she loved her three children, ages five through seven, and how she found fulfillment teaching her other children, the students at Parkview. I talk about Seve Vamara and Julie Smythe draping their bodies over their students as the gunman kept firing and firing and firing, Vamara and Smythe saving their students but making the ultimate sacrifice in the process.

I pause so I don't cry. I hope the country doesn't think this is theatrics. It isn't.

And then I go off script.

"I have two lists I am going to read to you. Please bear with me. The rest of the speech — and you'll just have to believe me on this — was much more exciting the way my speechwriter wrote it. But I'm not going for excitement. I'm going for importance, and I can't think of anything more important than the lists I am going to read to you."

One by one, I read the name of each child killed at Parkview.

"Jeremy Short. He was President of the Student Council. Sandra Seymour. She starred in the school play last year. Lupe Vasquez, the Homecoming Queen. John Wilson, an average C student voted by his fellow students as "most likely to wind up in in Hollywood and/or a wanted poster." Children. Children, damn it! Children who won't grow old, who won't raise other children, who won't laugh, love, cry because their lives ended yesterday."

It takes about 10 minutes to get through the list. Viewers might try to switch to another station, although that would be fruitless because I am on every station.

"The second list – and I know I am going to piss off Republicans and Democrats alike – are your senators and congressmen who have voted against common sense gun laws that would have prevented yesterday's tragedy and the countless tragedies we have endured through the years."

I start with the Democrats.

"Rance Herbert of West Virgina, Jason Ambert of Indiana, Collin Feeherty of Iowa, Orest Heart of Alabama..."

The second part of this list – the Republicans – is longer. Somehow, a lot of these people I considered as friends before this speech skipped over the part of the Constitution that guarantees life, liberty and the pursuit of happiness and went straight to the Second Amendment.

"Jeb Moline of Arizona, Sallie Schultz of California, James Green of Oregon, Steve Barnes of Iowa, Abigail Russell of Maine...."

I save Trey Collins of New Mexico for 10th. He could have been first because his state is No. 1 in mass shootings, but I don't want this to sound like a political speech directed at Collins.

Damn, it takes a long time to finish the second list. Damn, there are a lot of elected officials who don't listen to constituents who demand common sense gun laws.

"These congressmen and senators I just named, some of them are up for reelection," I conclude. "You have a vote. Use it because those children who died at Parkview yesterday, they'll never get a chance to use their votes. Think about them when you enter that ballot box."

Tarik, Aida, Jim and my closest advisors are thrilled backstage. But let's see what the networks tomorrow and the American public in November think about one of the most difficult speeches I have ever delivered.

CHAPTER 68

PNT liked it.

They actually managed to fit 10 people around a long table, the most I've ever seen on PNT. For a cable station tanking in the ratings, you'd think they would want to cut back on length-of-table overhead. But the tables get longer and longer and the ratings get smaller and smaller. If things continue at this rate, I'll only be dealing with DVTV and VOX in the future.

Ron Grey: "A historic moment. A president taking on guns while naming names, including members of his own party."

Ashcroft Smith: "What a breath of fresh air. We, as journalists, get tired of politicians spouting the same old, hackneyed expressions. President Pappas didn't give us the same old, hackneyed expressions. He has a bully pulpit and he used it to bully politicians on both sides of the aisle."

Gloria Berman: "But what will it mean for President Pappas in the general election? He has to win the swing states and last night's address, while it sounded good to us, might be a big swing and miss when it comes to winning over voters in Michigan and Wisconsin."

Gloria has it right. I always thought she did a good job and have wondered why PNT hasn't promoted her to a primetime spot. But she isn't young and the woman they just promoted to one of their primetime spots has two of the things you need for ratings: she is young and pretty. She doesn't have the third thing: knowledge. I guess PNT figures she'll grow into the job.

DVTV, albeit with a smaller table, liked what I did, too.

Bekka Mornay, twenty minutes into her patented monologue: "Imagine that. A president wanting to do the right thing. What a concept?"

Ari Melman: "It's like Tupac said, 'Reality is wrong. Dreams are for real.'" Ari's guest: "What does that mean, Ari?" Ari: "Just that President Pappas is dreaming big. Let's hope that the senators and congressman he called out last night help those dreams come true."

But I didn't win over the entire cable news market. My old buddy, Brolin Murphy, predictably panned my address.

"Clearly," he said, "President Pappas was making a political speech, and the target of his speech was Senator Collins. Forget all that talk about guns and deaths. Forget those pictures of the teachers on President Pappas' desk. Yes, those teachers are heroes. But President Pappas wasn't a hero for callously using their photos as props for a political campaign."

One of these nights, I'll ask Brolin out to dinner. To get back at him, I'll make him pick up the check.

But I don't expect Brolin or Collins to be my biggest critics the day after my address. I hear a knock on the Oval Office door and usher Patricia Paschall in.

"That was quite a stunt you pulled last night," Paschall says, still standing.

"Have a seat, Patricia, Want some coffee? A donut?"

"I'll stand. This shouldn't take long."

Paschall goes on to tell me that she took a huge political chance backing me as the Democratic nominee for President. She got pushback from many of her Democratic colleagues who wanted a lifelong Democrat to lead the ticket.

"But I fought for you, and I usually get what I want," Paschall says.

"Then, last night, you go out and trash Democrats who might be out of jobs come November because of what you said. Do you want a Republican House and Senate for your second term? Because that's what you'll get, assuming you win in November."

I don't tell Patricia that passing meaningful legislation is more important to me than winning a second term. I don't tell her that I named Democrats, too, because I didn't want my speech to look like a political ploy. Paschall is a political animal and, just like all the political animals on both sides of the aisle, winning comes first and issues – even one as important as passing sensible gun laws – come second.

"I apologize, Patricia."

"I'm not looking for apologies. I just want our party's nominee to start acting like a guy who isn't running as an Independent."

"No problem."

Patricia leaves in a huff.

I'm left wondering how I'm going to handle gun control when it comes up in my first debate with Collins next week.

CHAPTER 69

Islamic Jihad is the culprit two days later and is only too happy to claim responsibility for a pre-dawn attack on the border town of Jakub that left 87 killed, 147 injured and 97 hostages taken.

"Palestinians merely want to live in peace with all of the attendant rights enjoyed by the Zionists," new Islamic Jihad leader, Kafir Suleiman, broadcast from an unknown location. "This raid would not have taken place if the Zionist prime minister had not initiated a series of attacks that have left thousands of Palestinians dead. The blood is on the hands of the Zionist prime minister, not on the hands of our brave Islamic Jihad warriors."

Noah has been unrelenting on his attacks since the Haifa attack, demanding that the people responsible for the killings come forward before Israel relented. None came forward and Noah, true to his word, has leveled a good portion of southern Gaza while, at the same time, attempting to send food to innocent Palestinian civilians.

The food never reached its destination, Noah told me, because it was intercepted at the border by Islamic fundamentalists.

The food never reached its destination, Farid told me from his hiding place in central Gaza, because it never was sent.

"Enough!" I tell Noah and Farid when I finally arrange a three-way conference call the day after the most recent bombing. "Palestinians are dying. Israelis are dying. We have to find a way to a peaceful solution."

At this point, though, I don't know if that is possible. Fundamentalist

Islamic groups all over the Middle East have condemned the peace talks as a waste of time and proclaimed Sept. 11 as Martyr Day. The choice of Sept. 11 was no accident. Muslim leaders want to liken the Palestinian dead to the thousands of U.S. citizens who died in the attack on the World Trade Center on Sept. 11, 2001.

Noah wasn't in a negotiating mood before the most recent attack. He almost surely will get voted out of office because of what his opponents call "traitorous" leadership in negotiating with the Palestinians. If he goes out, though, it appears that he literally wants to go out with a bang.

"My political opponents might be right," he told me in a conversation we had last week. "I have been a fighter for Israeli freedom all of my life. When the stated goal of the Palestinian government is the annihilation of Israel, what else can I be? Then, for a brief moment I thought I could engineer a lasting peace. I can't sleep at night knowing that my weak moment has led to the death of so many of my people."

I appealed to Noah's sense of justice. Noah's sense of justice has changed, though.

I negotiated a temporary ceasefire with Noah after Haifa, threatening a cut in aid as a cudgel. The ceasefire seemed to be working, but Israel has enough firepower to level Gaza and the West Bank without U.S. help and, after the Islamic Jihad attacks, looks like it will start a crushing offensive soon.

"The world is starting to look at the Israelis as criminals," I told Noah during a recent conversation.

"The world – if I can borrow an old phrase I often heard on the playground at Central High in Philadelphia – can go fuck itself," Noah responded.

Which leaves us with more Israelis dead and, when Noah retaliates, more Palestinians dead.

"If I could capture Suleiman and deliver him to the Israeli Prime

Minister," Farid offers during the three-way call, "would that result in another ceasefire?"

Noah pauses. Farid already is anathema to many in his country. Delivering Suleiman to Noah would almost ensure his death.

"And you think that would bring a lasting peace?" Noah says.

"I am looking for a temporary peace," Farid says. "We can work on the lasting peace later."

CHAPTER 70

The first of my three nationally televised debates with Collins is two days from now and I want to get my head straight. So, I wait outside Dr. Carty's office for my pre-debate, getting-my-head-on-straight session. This makes two sessions in a week. If Eric didn't think I was crazy before, he thinks it now.

Unless, of course, Eric called this session to talk about deeper issues. But what, at this moment, can be deeper than kicking Collins's ass on national TV?

"Just be genuine," Eric says when we start. "That's most important."

"Unless, of course, Collins hits me with a shaky economy. Maybe I shouldn't be so genuine then."

Eric smiles, stands and places an old record on the turntable. It's Sam Cooke's classic, "A Change Is Gonna Come," something he used to play as background music when we first started seeing each other decades ago.

"And the meaning of the music is what?" I ask. "There will be a change in the White House? I'll have to change my tune, maybe stop being such a pain in the ass to the party that nominated me?"

"None of the above. I just like this song."

I haven't seen many therapists, so I don't know if Eric is unconventional. Let me amend that. I have seen a lot of therapists, but all of them lasted a session or two while Eric has lasted thirty years.

But I'm guessing most therapists don't play Sam Cooke during sessions.

"I don't want to talk about you today," Eric says. "I want to talk about myself."

"Isn't therapy supposed to be about me, not you?"

"Actually, it's about both of us. That's what a relationship is, isn't it?"

Eric goes on to tell me that he watched my Parkview speech on TV. He tells me that he agrees with my stance and thought I was genuine – there's that word again – when I talked about the kids and teachers who died. He also tells me that I might have been attempting political suicide when I named Democrats.

"The thing is," Eric says, "I was wrong. I probably have been wrong about you for a long time. We've talked about fear of failure forever. But something struck me during that speech. You don't fear failure. You fear doing the wrong thing."

"Thank you."

I came in here to get my head straight for the debates and Eric is apologizing. One of the many things I like about seeing him is that our sessions rarely go the way I expect.

"I'm just trying to be genuine," Eric says. "If you and I aren't honest with each other, we don't have a relationship. And being honest isn't a one-sided thing. It works both ways."

"What does that have to do with the debates?"

Eric takes Sam Cooke off the turntable and replaces him with Jeff Buckley singing Leonard Cohen's "Hallelujah."

"I know. I know," I say, beating Eric to the punch. "You just like this song."

"Actually, I prefer the K.D. Laing version."

Eric talks to me about debate preparations. I already know that Jim Banoff will play Collins, Aida Curtain will play the moderator and Tarik, as he's done for much of my life, will tell me when I screw up.

"Just be genuine on that stage. Be yourself," Eric says. "You've won a lot of elections. People might not always like your message, but they like the messenger."

"And if Collins asks me about the economy?"

"You genuinely lie your ass off."

CHAPTER 71

The site of the debate is Lewiston, Maine, most famous for hosting the second Ali – Liston fight in 1965, a fight in which Liston was knocked out in the first round by what most people called a "phantom" punch and what Ali later called his "anchor" punch.

I was seven years old at the time of that fight and couldn't see the punch that sent big, bad Sonny Liston down for the count. Fifty-nine years later, I still can't spot the punch on tape but have heard rumors that Liston was tied to the mob and might have thrown the fight.

Why Maine? I argued with Collins and the networks that it had never hosted a presidential debate before, that New England was a key region for both candidates in the upcoming election and that Mainers are particularly discerning folk. I didn't mention that it is one of my favorite vacation destinations and is the primary purveyor of my single favorite food: lobster. Collins agreed to the site. Maybe Collins loves lobster, too.

"He'll want to pull you into this is-he-too-crazy-to-be-President argument," Tarik tells me backstage as we wait for VOX, whose people are moderating this debate, to get the stage and crowd ready. "Don't take the bait."

"Is 'crazy' a clinical term?"

"What does that have to do with anything?"

"I don't think it is. He calls me crazy; I'll say it's not a clinical term and will win the all-important psychiatrist vote."

"You're whacked."

"Whacked. Another word, I'm guessing, that my esteemed opponent might trot out tonight."

Tarik didn't want Brolin Murphy as one of the moderators, considering how Murphy has used me as a punching bag leading up to the debate. I overrode Tarik. People don't like bullies. If Murphy tries to bully me, people won't like him and his favorite presidential candidate, Collins.

I insisted on the other moderator: Aenid Wallace. Wallace used to be fair-and-balanced when VOX touted itself as fair-and-balanced. His name still is associated with VOX even though he is long gone. It will look like me against the world when I'm on stage facing down Collins, Murphy and Wallace. Everybody loves an underdog, just like they loved heavy underdog Cassius Clay when he took down Liston in their first fight in 1964 before he changed his name to Muhammad Ali.

I don't plan to change my name after this debate, win or lose. And I don't plan to go down like Liston. Hopefully, Collins is sniffing the canvas.

"The first question, by flip of the coin, goes to Senator Collins," Murphy says after we take the stage. I wonder if they flipped to see who asked the first question. Nah. Murphy has the ratings and Wallace no longer is on VOX. "The rising crime rate that has plagued President Pappas throughout his tenure, what is your plan to do away with it?"

"An excellent question, Brolin, and you're right, crime has risen dramatically since Governor Pappas became President Pappas. Portland, Oregon, despite its decidedly liberal politics, used to be one of my favorite places to visit because of its many fine restaurants, it's youthful energy and because I was a Bill Walton fan, God rest his soul."

Collins wouldn't know Bill Walton if Walton dunked over him. Collins isn't a sports fan, unless you consider yachting a sport, and I doubt he even knows about Walton leading the Trailblazers over my beloved Philadelphia

76ers in the 1977 NBA Finals.

As for youthful energy, Collins doesn't have much chance of capturing the youth vote in Portland or anywhere this debate is being shown. But I have to give the man credit. He's trying.

"And Chicago, another one of the cities I used to love before President Pappas took office, has become the murder capital of the country. Wilmington, Philadelphia, just about any city with Democratic mayors soft on criminals, they also are hotbeds of crime."

"Thirty seconds," Murphy interjects.

Collins uses his remaining time to tick off the names of 10 American cities, all run by Democratic mayors, all with sky-high crime rates.

"President Pappas," Murphy says. "You have a minute to respond."

"I'm still waiting for Senator Collins to respond to your question which, if memory serves, asked my opponent to tell the American public what he would do about a crime rate which, the way he makes it sound, has gotten worse since I was elected President. I'll make this quick. One, crime actually is down in most states, Senator Collins's state being a notable exception. And, two, the guns I plan to reduce in the general population when I pass a comprehensive gun safety bill, will get into the hands of the people who should have them: the police."

Wallace is next.

"You have included the Palestinian leader in peace talks with Israel," Wallace says. "The man fought against the Israelis in the Six-Day and Yom Kippur wars. His party, Intifada, wants Israel wiped off the face of the Earth. If you really want peace, why bring a person who has spent his whole life engaging in war to the negotiating table?"

Collins is smiling. A heckler at the back of the auditorium yelling "From the River to the Sea" is escorted out of the room.

"Thank you for the question, Aenid," I start. "Believe me, I thought long and hard about allowing the leader of Intifada in on talks with America's great friend, Israel. And you are right. President Fadal has fought against Israelis all his life. But two things convinced me that President Fadal had to participate in talks that may lead to a lasting peace..."

From the back of the room, a man screaming "Death to Palestinians" is escorted out of the room.

"First," I continue, "it takes two parties to reach an agreement. I couldn't broker a peace without one of the parties – the leader of Palestine's government – sitting at the table. And, two, President Fadal has demonstrated to my satisfaction that he wants peace, a lasting peace. And we had it until a fringe group not affiliated with President Fadal engineered the Haifa bombing."

"Senator Collins, you have 30 seconds to respond."

I count the use of the word "enemy" five times during Collins's 30 seconds. Three of the references, by my count, were directed at Farid. Two were directed at me.

And so it went until the closing minutes when Senator Collins finally trotted out the B-word.

"He's bipolar, America," Collins said. "Do we really want a man with bipolar illness trying to broker a peace in the Middle East? Or trying to broker a traffic ticket, for that matter."

I smile.

"I've never gotten a traffic ticket in my life, Senator Collins. If you have a couple outstanding tickets, though, you are free to take it up with the Department of Justice. Before the election or after I win, it doesn't matter to me."

A few laughs and one audience member screaming for me to forgive his traffic tickets.

"As for my illness, Senator Collins, I am touched by your concern. In fact, I am touched by your concern every time you go on TV and ramble on about an illness you know little about.

"Sometimes, though, I think it's because you can't talk about your policies because you don't have any good policies. You certainly don't want to talk about your pro-gun stance when your state leads the nation in mass shootings. You certainly don't want to promote peace in the Middle East when you traffic in fear, not peace. But, hey, that's why America is the greatest democracy in the history of the world. People can go out and vote for a bipolar president who wants peace, not war. People can vote for a bipolar President who wants fewer guns, not more. Or they can vote for someone who doesn't have bipolar or, for that matter, a clue."

CHAPTER 72

Tarik and I have barely finished high-fiving backstage when the flash polls start rolling in.

PNT: A small sample of viewers thought Collins won the debate.

DVTV: Again, Collins came back the winner, particularly on the bipolar issue.

VOX: It was a runaway. Their flash poll had Collins wiping the floor with me. Murphy: "You saw the next president up there and it wasn't the guy who is president now."

"They're flash polls," Tarik says later. "The sample size is tiny. People go by their gut before they have a chance to really think about what you guys said. Wait until the real polls come out tomorrow."

The real polls are worse. I feel like Liston after he was pummeled in his first fight with Ali in Miami Beach. I'm not sure how Liston felt physically after the second fight in Maine – I'm pretty sure he was well-paid for taking a dive on that phantom punch – but our bottom line is the same: Liston and I lost.

"Fucking Murphy," Tarik says. "The guy is in Collins's pocket. You watch. Collins gets elected and Murphy is his Chief of Staff."

This is the first time I've heard Tarik mention the possibility of Collins winning, which puts him solidly in the camp of most of the people who watched the debate last night.

How could I have been so wrong? I thought I crushed Collins on the crime issue, that I handled the Middle East question well and pretty much outargued my opponent on most questions Murphy and Wallace threw our way.

More in-depth polls later in the week show why I was so wrong: the mental health issue. Three words out of Collins's mouth during his closing remarks -- "He's bipolar, America," -- pretty much washed away any gains I accumulated earlier in the debate.

I made this bed. I wanted America to know I was bipolar because mental illness is such an important and misunderstood issue in this country. I wanted to show that people with mental illness don't have to cower in the shadows like they did in the old days. I wanted to show that mental illness, just like physical illness, is treatable and people can succeed – hell, I'm President – if they acknowledge and treat their illness.

If early returns are an indication, though, I haven't succeeded in showing the American public that people can overcome mental illness and lead productive lives.

Maybe we're not so far removed from the old days. And maybe I'm not far removed from being an ex-President.

CHAPTER 73

My Secretary of State is doing a great job. To think, I was ready to replace James Mason after he argued against me in the 25th Amendment hearings. Now, he is my point man in Israel in the quest for peace in the Middle East.

Noah Abrams, with a nudge from Mason, has declared a temporary cease-fire. In exchange, Islamic Jihad released 20 of the 97 hostages taken in the Jakub massacre. Abrams won't commit to a permanent ceasefire, though, until all of the hostages are released and the Palestinian government changes its charter to reflect that it does not want Israel wiped off the face of the Earth.

"Your high school pal, Noah, is a tough customer," Mason told me the other day during a break from negotiations with Abrams.

"He has to be. Otherwise, there would be no Israel."

Mason also is spearheading an effort to get food to Palestinian civilians in Rafah, which was leveled by Israeli bombs last week. The U.S. plans to airdrop food to the civilians. Whether it finds its way into the hands of the people who need it most is another matter.

I've filled Mason in on Farid's promise to deliver Kafir Suleiman to Noah Abrams. But I haven't told Mason yet about my conversation with Farid yesterday. Farid says two of his men have infiltrated the Islamic Jihad network and there is a chance – although Farid is taking a bigger chance with his life – that he will be able to capture the Islamic Jihad leader.

Getting Suleiman would be big. Assuming Farid lives through this, transforming Intifada and eliminating Islamic Jihad completely would be bigger. There still is a chance for peace, but I'm not banking on it. I'd have to be crazy – oops; technically, I am – to think I could be instrumental in bringing peace to people who haven't known, or even wanted, peace for centuries.

"Let me ask you something," I say before ending my daily call with Mason. "Did you want me out as president?"

"Nothing personal," Mason says. "But my allegiance is to the Constitution first and to you second. I wanted a president who could perform his duties under the Constitution."

"You didn't think I could perform my duties under the Constitution?"

Silence.

More silence.

And finally: "There's a little static on this end, Mr. President. I'll have to call you back later."

CHAPTER 74

I feel for Morris Platner. I really do. His son was killed by a terrorist on what was supposed to be the happiest day of his life, his wedding, and Platner never will forget.

If something like that ever happened to Lin, I don't know what I would do to the person I held responsible. Actually, I do. Ariana would have to visit me in prison.

Unfortunately, I am the person Morris Platner holds responsible for his son's death. I am the one who initiated peace talks. The mass shooter who killed Morris' son, according to the FBI, wanted revenge, revenge on all Jewish people, and got it in the form of Morris' son and 122 others killed at Temple Beth Shalom.

"It's not your fault," Ariana tells me every time I watch Platner rail against me during one of the Republican Vice-Presidential nominee's speeches.

"Intellectually, I know that. Maybe my heart will come around someday."

Morris still walks with a limp as a result of the shooting. It is noticeable whenever he takes the stage to blast me for what he considers my "foolhardy" attempts to bring peace to the Middle East.

"You don't negotiate with terrorists," Platner says at a campaign rally televised by PNT. "Terrorists understand one language: retaliation. President Pappas doesn't understand that language. He doesn't understand what it feels like to lose a child."

I want to tell Morris that I am working hard to forge a lasting peace in the Middle East so other Israelis and Palestinians won't die. I want to tell him that I grieve for his son, too, and also won't forget the Temple Beth Shalom shooting for the rest of my life.

But I can't. We are opponents in a political race. Maybe I'll tell him later. Maybe I'll finally stop blaming myself, much like Morris is blaming me, for Jacob Platner's death.

Today, though, I just listen.

"President Collins and I won't be so accommodating to the terrorists," Morris says. "A terrorist kills 10 Jews, we'll kill 100 terrorists in return. A terrorist wants to wipe out the State of Israel, President Collins and I will team with our good friend, Israeli Prime Minister Noah Abrams, to wipe out the terrorists."

Platner and Collins's rhetoric isn't playing well on college campuses around the country. There have been numerous pro-Palestinian demonstrations fueled, in part, by college presidents who refuse to call genocide against the Jews hate speech.

Overwhelmingly, though, the U.S. is pro-Israel. But I don't know how long it will last if Noah resumes his unrelenting bombing of Palestine.

"A heart-wrenching speech from a man who has suffered an incomprehensible personal loss," Jack Tanner says after Platner finishes.

"People -- President Pappas, in particular – overcomplicate this," Brolin Murphy says. "Swords, not accords. Level Palestine. It's hard to have an Israel-Palestine problem when one of the combatants no longer exists."

Tarik grabs two beers and hands me one as we watch TV in the Oval Office.

"What are you going to do, because you have to do something?" Tarik says.

"I'll keep negotiating."

Tarik takes a swig of his beer.

"A noble stance," he says.

"Thank you."

"And a losing one."

CHAPTER 75

ongressman Dick Dulin of Illinois is my gun safety point man in the House. His career as a congressman is even longer than my decades-long career as a Mayor/Governor/President and won't end anytime soon if it's up to his constituents.

"It will end when I end," Dulin tells me as I meet with him and Tarik in the Oval Office today. "Three bypass surgeries, one bout with cancer and a liver transplant. I would have been worm food a long time ago if it weren't for the miracles of modern medicine."

Dulin is affectionately called "The Shepherd" by his colleagues and is one of the few remaining Congressmen who actually believes in compromise. The longest-tenured Democrat in Congress has shepherded a number of bills through the House, some of which have actually make it through the Senate, because he believes in getting things done, not in getting things "right" as defined by whoever is saying they are right.

And that is why we were able to pass the most comprehensive gun control bill in the nation's history last year. Dulin got enough of his Republican colleagues in the House to cross the aisle by compromising on a number of portions of the bill. Then, after it went to the Senate, Dulin relied on the relationships he has built over the years and more than a little arm-twisting to turn the proposed bill into law.

But it isn't enough, which is why I asked Dulin to see me today. We still need to beef up background checks. We still need to keep guns out of the hands of domestic abusers. And we still need a total ban on assault weapons, which have been responsible for nearly half of the deaths and 80 percent of the injuries in mass shootings in the U.S. over the last seven years.

"Don't know if I can help you on assault rifles," Dulin says. "They call me 'The Shepherd.' They don't call me 'The Magician.' Some folks think the Second Amendment gives them a right to own nuclear weapons."

"The hell with them," Tarik says.

"That, Tarik, is why I wanted Dick to meet with us today. This isn't like you elbowing me to win a game of one-on-one. Elbow those Congressmen, they elbow you back hard and nothing gets done."

I give Dulin the 10-point plan I've been working on with my gun safety experts. Dulin looks at it, shakes his head and promises to do his best when the Republican-controlled House convenes again next week.

Tarik is hunkered down on the sofa after Dulin leaves, gulping down his third cup of coffee and looking like he spent last night going one-on-one with a bottle of rum.

"You need to take it easy, my friend," I say.

"With you down double-digits in the polls? I'm too old to look for another job."

"We've come back from worse."

Tarik already knew that, but still doesn't look happy.

"What's bothering you?" I ask.

"Rachel is going back to Israel."

"Did you screw things up again?"

Tarik gets up and pours a drink much stronger than coffee: mezcal, straight up.

"Isn't it a little early for that?"

"Early for mezcal but it's getting late in the campaign. This could be our last rodeo, partner."

"You didn't answer my initial question. Did you screw things up?"

Tarik downs his drink and pours another shot.

"One of those hostages they took at Jakub. It was Rachel's brother. Her family needs her."

I have never seen Tarik shed a tear over a woman. Hell, I've never heard him admit to an emotion stronger than "she's alright."

But Tarik looks shaken now.

"I was falling in love," he says. "What did I tell you? It's better to be alone. No one can hurt you."

"Or make you happy, either."

Tarik wipes a tear from his eye and gets out of his chair.

"Fuck it. We have an election to win. And a gun bill to pass. Time for me to twist a few arms."

"Take a few days off, Tarik. Regroup. I'll get somebody to pick up the slack."

"The hell you will. You need me. And I need something to take my mind off Rachel."

My best friend leaves to twist arms and try to put Rachel in his rear-view mirror. With Tarik and Dulin doing the heavy lifting, maybe, just maybe, this gun bill will pass.

And if it fails in the Senate with Collins voting against it, I'll have something else to use against him.

CHAPTER 76

Mason calls from Tel Aviv the next day and tells me that the cease-fire won't last. He has pulled out all of the stops, including the possibility that the U.S. might cut aid to Israel if Noah doesn't extend the cease-fire, but the Israeli Prime Minister isn't budging.

"He might be the most stubborn person I've ever met, present company excluded," Mason says.

I certainly can see Noah's point. Islamic Jihad has refused to release more hostages, most of whom are women and children, unless Noah releases captured Islamic Jihad members. It isn't close to an apples-to-apples thing. Terrorists for innocents? Noah shouldn't cave.

But Israel's status in the world community is plummeting. Israel did not start this latest war, but they certainly are finishing it even though they are facing another one – Nakbar from the North – that has been ratcheting it up for several weeks. Many more Palestinians than Israelis have died and the world, with few exceptions, is looking at Israel as the bad guy. The U.N. wanted to charge Israel with war crimes, but the U.S. vetoed the action.

I reach Noah by secure phone later.

"Just a few more weeks?" I ask. "Mason thinks he is making headway on the hostages."

"Your Secretary of State doesn't know these people like I do. And I'm supposed to be mollified by the return of hostages who wouldn't be hostages if Islamic Jihad didn't take them in the first place?"

U.S. humanitarian efforts have had mixed results. Yes, some of the food we've dropped into Palestine is reaching innocent Palestinians guilty of nothing more than being Palestinian. But most of the food, my sources tell me, is finding its way into terrorist hands. The same goes for medical supplies U.S. and U.N. forces have sent.

What to do? What to do? I'm not the first U.S. President who has spent sleepless nights pondering the Middle East dilemma, and I won't be the last if my efforts fail.

And then I get an encrypted message from Farid later that night that gives me a glimmer of hope.

"Getting close to Suleiman," it says. "One week."

I'd gladly give him a week, but I'm not pulling the military strings. Noah is.

The Middle East, the gun control bill and my reelection bid have me more anxious than I've been in a long, long while.

"Take your meds and you'll be alright. Take your meds and you'll be alright."

Eric's voice has been resonating in my head a lot lately, and I've paid attention to his admonition.

I just hope it's enough.

CHAPTER 77

Dick Dulin didn't have to be a magician. Not even close. Oh, he managed to get a few Republicans to vote for my beefed- up gun control bill, but it wasn't necessary.

The bill passed the House, 57-42, with one Congressman absent. That Congressman, Jerry White, hails from New Mexico where, I assume, he plays golf with New Mexico Senator Trey Collins whenever he gets a chance. He must have been golfing the day of the vote.

The Parkview school shooting clearly has touched a nerve. At least, in the House. A total ban on assault weapons was unthinkable a year ago. Another mass shooting engineered by yet another assault rifle-toting murderer turned out to be more thinkable this time.

What surprised me even more than the vote, though, were the speeches – more like diatribes – a few of the Congressmen made on C-Span that were rebroadcast on all of the major networks.

Josh Harter, Democrat, New Jersey: "If this bill doesn't get through the Senate, we're doomed. Hopefully, Senator Collins is paying attention."

Bernard Gelfin, Democrat, New Hampshire: "Anyone in the Senate with a conscience will vote for this bill. The question is, does Senator Collins have a conscience?"

Susan Harris, Democrat, Virginia: "No more blood, Senator Collins. It will be on your hands."

Tarik and I are playing one of our intermittent games of one-on-one shortly after the vote. The games have become more intermittent because of the campaign, because of the gun bill and because of the crisis we're dealing with in the Middle East.

My aching knees and Tarik's aching back also have something to do with it.

"You're about to lose, Evan," Tarik says, dribbling the ball at the top of the key and holding a five-basket lead.

"Are we talking basketball, elections or gun safety votes?"

"The basketball game's a given. The election and the gun bill? You actually have a shot."

Tarik, all gloom and doom before the House vote, has been more upbeat lately. Internal polling numbers have been trending my way.

I'm thinking it's something else, though.

"Rumor has it," I say just before Tarik fakes left, goes right and buries a jumper to beat me, "that you had lunch with Josh Harter shortly before the gun bill came up for a vote."

"It isn't a rumor," Tarik says as we towel off. "The Diplomat. You ought to try it sometime. The best bacon, lettuce and tomato sandwiches I've ever had."

"And you talked about?"

"BLTs. Harter thinks they use too much mayonnaise. I think they're perfect."

Tarik also admits that he had lunch before the House vote with Gelfin and Harris.

"Gelfin also thinks they use too much mayo, but what does he know?"

"Enough to blast Collins in his speech. How about Harris?"

"The woman is a BLT afficionado. She agrees with me completely."

"About the BLT or about the need to skewer the man who stands between me and a second term in the White House?"

Tarik just smiles. His work – damn good work – has taken his mind off Rachel.

"You know, you need to work on your game, Evan. Time was, you used to beat me."

"Time was, you didn't promise things to politicians when you don't have the power to promise them anything."

Tarik pretends that he is hurt. One of these days I'll mention a tell – he scratches his left ear lobe when he isn't telling the truth – which has allowed me to relieve him of much of his salary during our White House poker games.

"I merely promised them my undying gratitude. And yours, too."

If I lose the election, I'll miss the White House basketball games, Tarik schmoozing politicians, and the idea that two boys from West Philly grew up to be two of the most powerful men in the world.

I won't give myself a chance to miss Tarik, though. Wherever I go, I want him to go with me.

CHAPTER 78

It's Presidential Debate II time. I sure hope it goes better than Presidential Debate I when Collins waited until his closing remarks to make his bipolar comment and reaped the benefits by getting a seven-point bump in the polls the following week.

But a lot has changed in the month since then.

The gun bill has garnered almost universal acclaim, DVTV calling it the "Stop the Carnage Bill," and PNT running a scroll beneath each newscast unfavorably comparing the number of assault rifle deaths in the U.S. to those in Great Britain, Australia and other countries that don't permit assault rifles. VOX pretty much has remained neutral which, to me, speaks louder than anything.

The ceasefire, much to my surprise, continues in the Middle East. Noah and Farid are talking again, and Israel's Prime Minister is holding out hope that Farid will lead him to Suleiman, that Islamic Jihad will be dismantled, and that Farid will be able to restructure the Palestinian government so that it at least tolerates and, most importantly, doesn't attack Israel.

Jobs are up, inflation is going down, and Collins's lead has shrunk to four percentage points as we stand backstage waiting for the debate to begin at New York's Lincoln Center.

I spy Collins in the corner, walk over and shake his hand.

"May the best man win," I say.

"I don't think you want that to happen."

"Come on, Trey. Be nice. And wipe that crumb off your lip."

I see Collins try to wipe an imaginary crumb off his lip as I leave. Score one for me, although I don't think it'll earn any extra votes.

DVTV is hosting this debate. I didn't object to Murphy at the first debate, in part, because I wanted to look like I was being bullied. The larger part, though, was getting Collins to agree to a quid pro quo: Bekka Mornay and Ari Melman moderating our second debate. Mornay extols my virtues so much every night that Ariana has asked if Bekka and I are having an affair. And Melman has started squeezing a couple of Bonnie Raitt lyrics in with his rap lyrics, "as a tribute to President Pappas."

"I thought you did well last time, but you ended up tanking in the polls." Here's Tarik again, trying to boost my confidence pre-debate in a screwed up, Philly playground way. "I don't know what to tell you."

"How about 'good luck?' "

"Okay, good luck. You'll need it."

Melman explains the rules of the debate to the crowd and to the millions of people who will be watching on TV just two months before the election.

Mornay introduces us.

And we're off, me first.

"Thank you, America," I start as I look out over the packed house. "Thank you, DVTV, for holding this debate. And thank you, Senator Collins, for showing up. It would have been really tough debating if I was up here by myself."

The crowd laughs.

I start.

"I'm bipolar." There's a buzz in the crowd, and it's not because I am bipolar. Everybody knows that. It's because I made it my lead story to disarm Collins.

"Just thought I'd get that out of the way up front for two reasons. One, it'll leave Senator Collins with nothing to say the rest of the night. And, two, I wanted to discuss the difference between bipolar and crazy. Bipolar is an illness which, as I've demonstrated since I was diagnosed over 30 years and multiple winning elections ago, can be treated. I'm keeping up with treatment and, in my ever-so-slightly biased opinion, am serving this country well.

"Crazy, unlike bipolar, isn't a clinical term. So, I'll offer my definition. Crazy is when you vote time and time again for assault rifles, the type of weapon that killed all of those children at Parkview. Crazy is when you want to fuel the conflict in the Middle East. Crazy is building walls and promoting racism and dividing America."

Collins fumbles with his notes. I assume he was going to lead with my bipolar illness, but I beat him to the punch.

So, Collins goes Dan Quayle on me. Lloyd Bentsen, in a Vice-Presidential debate with Quayle way back in 1988, said "Jack Kennedy was a friend of mine; Senator, you're no Jack Kennedy" after Quayle had compared his experience favorably to Kennedy.

Collins's opening statement is Dan Quayle, word for word, in Quayle's response to Bentsen: "Mr. President, that was uncalled for."

Quayle wasn't considered the brightest bulb and not only because of that debate. He misspelled "potato" on national TV, and many thought he would be the anchor that dragged President George Bush to defeat.

But he didn't. Bush and Quayle won in a landslide.

Hopefully, Collins's Quayle-like performance at the beginning and throughout the night doesn't result in a similar result.

CHAPTER 79

I don't pay close attention to the usual media suspects the following week, although Tarik clues me in every day that they are singing my praises.

"Are you paying DVTV?" Tarik asks during one of our meetings. "I mean, all they do 24 hours a day is replay what they're calling your 'Bipolar, Not Crazy,' speech. And that Bekka Mornay. Are you sleeping with her?"

"That's what Ariana asks."

"Well, are you?"

PNT also is over the top, although not as much as DVTV. Tanner used one of his newscasts to delve into the presidencies of the handful of presidents who reportedly struggled with mental illness. Two of them, Teddy Roosevelt and John Adams, had bipolar.

"But no President, ever, has had the courage to come out with it on national TV during an election year, the way President Pappas did months ago," Tanner said. "And no President has gotten a political boost from mental illness the way President Pappas got a political boost after the second debate."

Even Murphy gave me a grudging nod on VOX.

"He is crazy," Murphy said. "Like a fox."

Collins's lead over me is down to two percentage points, according to an average of 10 polls. Filmmaker Michael Morehouse, who correctly predicted my longshot victory last time, is predicting another victory in

November.

But I'm not paying attention to cable news outlets at the breakfast table today. I'm paying attention to Lin, who is on break after acing all but one class – I'll have to get one of my Secret Servicemen to talk to that teacher – at Northwestern.

"I'm proud of you, Dad," Lin says. "And it isn't because you're going to win again."

"First," I say, passing the scrambled eggs, "Let's not jinx the election. And, second, I'm proud of you, too. All As, one B and I hear you're one of the best debaters on the debating team. Remember how you couldn't get on stage with your social anxiety?"

"Are you going with me to the mental health rally?"

"I'm thinking about it."

"Think hard. It's in two hours."

The Mental Health Awareness Rally was hastily put together after the second debate and will be held in front of the Lincoln Memorial this morning. Lincoln, not coincidentally, reportedly suffered from depression.

Psychology Today, the most widely read psychology magazine, has been touting the rally as "historic and long overdue." Counseling Today, one of the other top psychology publications, has called it the "Bipolar, Not Crazy" rally.

Andrea Shelton will be there. I didn't know who Andrea was until DVTV ran a piece on her Wednesday. She is from Kentucky, has been in and out of abusive relationships all her life, suffered from bipolar and tried to take her life last year.

"I always knew something was wrong," Andrea told DVTV reporter Glen Laury. "But everybody just told me to buck up, that I wasn't trying hard enough."

One of Andrea's boyfriends moonlighted as a psychiatrist when he wasn't beating the hell out of her. He told her that she had bipolar, Andrea sought the opinion of another psychiatrist, and she has done well after starting weekly counseling and taking daily meds. She even worked up the courage to kick out the abusive psychiatrist boyfriend, who subsequently lost his license when another abused girlfriend reported him to the psychiatric board.

"You haven't answered my question," Lin says. "Are you going to join us at the rally?"

Do I want to keep throwing my illness in voters' faces? It's only part of who I am, albeit a big part. Do I want voters to think it's the only part?

"Okay. I'll be there with you."

CHAPTER 80

Somehow, Patricia Paschall managed to get the gun bill to the floor of the Senate shortly after it passed the House. There's a reason why people call her the best Senate minority or majority leader the Democrats ever had.

She gets things done.

But nothing Paschall can do will get this gun bill, a beefed-up gun control measure meant to prevent the type of human devastation we had at Parkview, through the Senate. The gun lobby is powerful, more Senators and Congressmen bowing at the altar of the NRA than listening to the people they are supposed to serve.

Why else would all of those good folks, and I use the word "good" advisedly, keep voting to keep assault rifles alive when assault rivals leave so many dead? Why else would those same Senators and Congressmen keep voting against sensible gun laws, using the Second Amendment as a protective cloak, when most of their constituents want stricter gun laws?

"Can you imagine if the Pez lobby was as strong as the gun lobby?" Tarik asks me.

"Pez?"

"You know, those cute little candies they jam into those cute little dispensers. I used to go out with a woman who collected Pez dispensers, but I didn't know she collected them until she finally let me into her apartment. She had shelves and shelves of Pez dispensers lined up against her wall. I couldn't get out of there fast enough."

"The one time you didn't sleep with a date."

"Oh, I slept with her. But I ran out of there five minutes later."

Tarik could be the worst political advisor in the world, but I'd keep him around because he makes me laugh. God knows, I need to laugh to keep from crying when I think of the prospect of Collins in the White House and an assault rival in every child's bookbag.

But there's an outside – very outside – chance that the Senate passes this bill. Since Parkview, Michigan passed a bill making it illegal to carry handguns in public. A Detroit gun manufacturer is challenging the constitutionality of the bill in the Supreme Court even as gun deaths in his own city have plummeted since it was implemented.

Arizona has beefed up its background check requirements. Florida is considering a bill that would make it illegal for a person who has been convicted of domestic abuse to buy guns. And Texas, where parents of the children murdered at Parkview have been featured daily in local newspapers and TV ads, has banned assault rifles. All of these bills are wending their way to the U.S. Supreme Court but, for the time being, gun-related deaths in these states are down.

"It's a small sample size," Collins said the other day during one of his many "Save The Gun" speeches. "Save the Gun." It's a term coined by the far-right fringe of the Republican Party. I have a raft of ads coming out in the near future featuring grainy videos of pro-gun advocates carrying "Save the Gun" placards in the background while not-so-grainy safer gun law people carry "Save the Children" placards in the foreground.

"President Pappas wakes up every morning trying to come up with ways to take away your Second Amendment rights," Collins told Chuck Merceir the other day on Meet the Press. "What's next? The First Amendment, the Third Amendment, the 14th amendment. I swear, this guy throws darts every day at an amendment dart board. Wherever the dart lands, that's the amendment he wants to eliminate."

Merceir, who probably is in my camp, snickered at that one. Ariana, who definitely is in my camp, couldn't stop laughing.

"Collins has charisma," Ariana said.

"So did Mussolini."

I set aside all of Thursday to watch the gun vote on PNT. There's nothing more boring than watching senators vote for a bill, but Tarik is here with me and we're chowing down on chips, guacamole and pizza. That'll make this loss easier to take.

Halfway through the guacamole, though, I am starting to think the bill might pass. It's 25-25, pretty much down party lines, with a number of senators from states that voted for me last election left to cast their votes.

"Serious question," Tarik says. "You have your choice of this bill passing and you losing the election, or this bill going down in flames with you winning the election, which do you pick?"

"This bill passing."

"Really?

"Really."

"Funny thing is, I believe you."

It's 50-49 against the bill with only one person, Senator Wilhelm from Idaho, left. Wilhelm's state is pro-gun, but he is one of the more progressive Republicans in the Senate.

If Wilhelm votes for the bill, it's tied 50-50 and my vice-president breaks the tie by passing the bill. The cameras are trained on Wilhelm as he uses up his allotted time to vote, shuffling through papers, having a heated conversation with a pro-gun Senator seated next to him and, finally, standing.

"The Chair recognizes the distinguished Senator from Idaho," the Senate majority leader intones.

Can a bill that will save so many lives and likely cost Senator Wilhelm his seat?

"I vote neigh," Wilhelm says.

The bill fails. Wilhelm will retain his seat.

Somewhere in that room, Senator Collins is smiling. I doubt that he will be smiling at our final debate when I paint him as a Senator who, because he voted against the bill, ensured that another Parkview is in our not-too-distant future.

CHAPTER 81

Turns out that Noah and Farid have been negotiating a peace treaty on their own without telling me. The talks started again after Kafir Suleiman experienced, according to Farid, "an unfortunate demise."

Farid had been holed up in a safe house in the small town of Rampah, five miles from the Gaza-Israel border. He had a small armed guard and one of his advisors, Khalafi Shardoom in the house, with barely enough food to exist.

"Islamic Jihad would have killed me if they knew where I was," Farid tells me during a conference call on the double-encrypted secure line in the Oval Office this morning. "The fewer people who know where I am, the better. And, with all due respect, that includes Americans."

Farid did alert Noah of his whereabouts, though. Go figure. One is Israeli. One is Palestinian. But they somehow managed to forge an alliance through our negotiations based on a shared desire: peace for their people.

Farid, with the help of Mossad intelligence agents, crossed into Israel two weeks ago. Al Jazeera is reporting that he is "missing and probably a victim of "Zionist treachery." Only a few of Noah's closest advisors know of Farid's whereabouts. If word leaked out that the Israeli Prime Minister and Farid were talking, Noah tells me, Israeli police would have taken Farid into custody, Noah would be replaced by a more militant member of the Knesset and peace would be unattainable.

"We have the biggest and best intelligence agency in the world," I tell Noah and Farid during our conference call. "How did you guys manage to pull this off without me knowing?"

"Because you are the biggest, not the best," Noah says. "When this is over, I will allow your CIA to undergo training directed by the head of Mossad. All of those security leaks you have been plagued by, Mr. President, they will go away."

Farid and Noah lay out the basics of their plan. But they are just the basics. The details still must be ironed out.

It includes an education program in Palestine conducted by a mixture of Israeli and Palestinians teachers, a detail Farid and Noah are still working on. Palestinian children, taught by fundamentalist teachers under lax U.N. supervision, have learned since they could walk that Israeli is the devil and must be eliminated. That would change but it will take a long time.

"For a lasting peace to exist," Farid says, "we have to change the way people think. It won't happen overnight, but my people need to stop thinking of Israelis as evil. Plus, Israel's military dwarfs ours. Why continue fighting an army you cannot beat?"

The plan also is contingent on Farid resuming his role as head of the Palestinian government and the elimination of the radical wing that controls the party in his absence.

"I trust him," Noah says. "Which is more than I can say for any Palestinian leader in the past. But the Palestinians cannot know that Israel played any part in Farid regaining power."

The Palestinian government charter, calling for the elimination of Israel, would be changed. Palestinians plotting attacks on Israel, Farid says, would be imprisoned or put to death. And Israelis plotting attacks on Palestine, Noah says, would be jailed.

Farid has promised to release Israeli hostages once he regains power.

Noah has promised to funnel food and medical supplies into Gaza when Farid is back on top.

"With Farid in power, I'll know that the food is getting into the hands of the civilians," Noah says. "Not into the hands of terrorists who will feast on our food before biting off the hand that feeds them."

Noah is taking a political chance. As a moderate, he is in the minority in a Knesset that only wants to use military means.

Farid literally is betting his life but is willing to take the chance.

"Many Palestinians will look at me as a traitor," he says. "I look at this as the only way to end the killing and, eventually, the only way Palestinians can achieve peace, prosperity and independence."

Peace, prosperity and independence. One is a long shot. Vegas would set long odds on all three coming to pass.

But Noah and Farid are working together. That's a step in the right direction, something that hasn't happened since the war began.

"And, Mr. President," Noah says before ending the call, "do not take it personally if you do not hear from us in a while. We have been doing quite well without you."

Yes, they have.

"Plus," Farid adds, "you have an election to win. I've seen your American polls. You should pay more attention to them."

CHAPTER 82

I was terrible when I first broadcast football games in college. Every time I talked into the microphone, I envisioned thousands of fans in their living rooms hanging on my every word, most of which I tripped over.

A broadcasting colleague told me of a mind game he played when he was on the air. He envisioned talking to one person, not thousands. He became a better broadcaster when he started doing it and so did I.

I played the same mind game after losing my first jury trial at the Philadelphia District Attorney's office. I stumbled over my words during that first case because, in my head, I was talking to 12 jurors and not the one person seated in the witness box. Once I whittled my audience down to one witness, my job became easier, my questioning became more conversational, and I had a 97 percent conviction rate by the time I left the D.A.'s office.

Tonight, at the third and final presidential debate, I will be talking to one person. We'll be using a Town Hall format and I'll be speaking to the one person from the audience PNT moderators Anderson Holder and Jack Tanner select to ask a question. It's why I like town hall debates.

"You realize, though, that there will be millions tuning in," Tarik tells me as we stand backstage.

"Are you trying to make me nervous?"

"No, I'm trying to reign you in. One-on-one, you're liable to say anything. Like in that gubernatorial debate, same format as tonight, you swore you were Zeus and a couple of other Greek gods combined."

"That was a long time ago, and I was off my meds."

"Just don't go Greek god on me tonight. You'll lose the election."

Forty people are in the audience at Swarthmore College in suburban Philadelphia. All are uncommitted voters screened by Gallup's research and polling people. Half of the questions will come from audience members. Half of the questions will come from social media. I just hope Holder and Tanner don't ask me about my alleged penchant for sleeping with five Ritz crackers under my pillow every night, something that popped up – probably masterminded by a 12-year-old in his basement -- on Twitter/X recently.

"The first questioner is Sarah McBride, a freshman at Swarthmore, and it goes to Senator Collins," Holder says.

This is good. Swarthmore might be one of the most liberal colleges in the country and the students can't like Collins's policies.

"The Senate came within one vote of passing the most comprehensive gun control legislation in history recently," McBride says. "It came down to one vote and you voted against it. Will you take responsibility when the next mass shooting occurs?"

I love Sarah McBride.

"Thank you, Sarah," Collins says. I'm guessing he doesn't love Sarah McBride. "And I agree that one of the candidates up here will bear partial responsibility if another mass shooting occurs. But that candidate won't be me. It will be President Pappas, who has forgotten to compromise along the way. If he put a sensible bill, not a wildly partisan bill, in front of the Senate, I assure you that I would have voted for it."

As opposed to all of those less partisan bills you voted down, Trey? I don't think so.

"And now, a question for President Pappas," Tanner says. "It comes from Rocco, a contractor from Philadelphia.

A big, beefy man takes the mike.

"President Pappas," he says. "A number of my family members suffer from mental illness. I love every one of them and do all I can to help, financially and with as much emotional support as I can provide. I don't know whether I'd want them as my President, though. Can you convince me and all of those other undecided voters to vote for a candidate with an admitted mental illness as opposed to a candidate who is not mentally ill?"

I tell him that I control my mental illness by taking meds and doing all of the other things you are supposed to do. I tell him to look at my record and to vote against me if he doesn't like my policies, but undecided voters should not make a decision based on a disability I have under control.

"FDR was one of the greatest, maybe *the* greatest President this country ever had, and he had serious physical challenges," I say. "But he got this country through the Great Depression and World War II. His cousin, Teddy Roosevelt, had bipolar. Through my three years as president, through my terms as Pennsylvania governor and Philadelphia's mayor, I have dealt well with many national and international crises while accepting and conquering my own personal challenges."

We move to internet concerns including – surprisingly -- the Great Ritz Cracker uproar. Holder brought it up, I'm sure, because he wanted a laugh to counter an unsmiling demeanor that costs him in the ratings.

He gets his laughs. The question won't help my chances of winning a second term, but it might help Holder in the ratings wars.

We close with Irv Lerner, a senior at Swarthmore who directs his question to me.

"I'm Jewish, Mr. President," he says. "My grandparents died in the holocaust. My parents and I deal almost daily with anti-Semitism which, as you know, has been on the rise in this country. But I'm also American. And I also want to minimize – no, to end -- the war in the Middle East. What have you done, what are you doing, to make sure the war ends, to make sure all of this killing stops?"

I can't tell him of my recent talks with Farid and Noah, although letting the nation know about the progress they've made certainly would buoy my chances at the presidency.

"First, I am sorry for your grandparents, and I am horrified by the anti-Semitism that has skyrocketed in this country, culminating in the massacre at Temple Beth Shalom," I say.

"Unfortunately, I can't be specific on ongoing talks with Palestinian and Israeli leaders which, hopefully, will bring a lasting peace in the Middle East. I will say this, though: I am very optimistic."

Lerner shakes his head. Clearly, he wants specifics and is not satisfied.

But there is nothing more specific I could say. Hopefully, the rest of the nation watching this town hall and all of the voters who go to the polls in a few weeks won't hold my evasive answer against me.

CHAPTER 83

I t's the silly season for political attack ads put out by independent political action committees, although it's not so silly for people getting paid to write those ads and certainly not so silly for people who believe those ads and vote accordingly.

The "Clueless Trey" PAC is running an ad showing an actor playing Trey Collins handing out guns to students, teachers and custodians, telling them not to use them unless somebody *"really, really scary"* walks through the front door. The most ridiculous part comes at the end. It's the actor laughing maniacally, kind of like the killer in a horror movie before he chops somebody's head off.

"The laugh," Ariana says as we watch from our bedroom one night. "It sounds more like you than Collins."

"Only when you're cooking Grandma's Surprise."

"Lin likes it."

"Crime-Loving Evan," not to be outdone by "Clueless Trey," is running an ad of me handing out guns to actor/prisoners at a prison in Philadelphia. It looks like Eastern State Penitentiary in Philadelphia, which truly is scary. Al Capone did time there. It's used as a Halloween attraction now and scares the hell out of visitors paying $20 a pop.

"Remember that time when you almost jumped out of your skin waiting in line to get in?" Ariana asks.

"You'd jump out of your skin, too, if something you thought was a vase of roses turned into a head and started howling at you."

"Such a brave man."

My favorite, though, is an ad sponsored by a group calling itself "One Flew Over the President's Nest." I guess they couldn't get Jack Nicholson, who played the title role in *One Flew Over the Cuckoo's Nest,* so they got an actor who gets lobotomized at the end of the ad.

"Do they still do lobotomies?" Ariana asks.

"I don't know."

"Maybe you can get one the next time I make Grandma's Surprise. I wouldn't have to listen to you complain so much."

The normal ads – the ones approved by the Democratic and Republican parties – are more serious. And more boring. They talk about infrastructure and taxes and inflation and probably put people to sleep before Collins and I say we approve of these messages.

But they are coming fast and furious as we head into the stretch of an election that most news outlets say is too close to call.

"How can it be too close to call?" Ariana asks during one of my increasingly frequent sleepless nights. "Collins is wrong about guns. He's wrong about everything."

"But he doesn't have bipolar. I do, and that's not going away anytime soon."

CHAPTER 84

With all that has been going on in the Middle East, with the debates, with campaigning all over the country and with trying to get Ariana to watch mob movies with me rather than those sleep-inducing English period pieces she loves so much, it's a wonder I haven't had a serious depression or gone off on a manic tangent.

Actually, it's not a wonder. I'm taking my meds and doing everything else Dr. Carty wants me to do. He should give me a gold star, I'm thinking, as I walk into his office.

"I won't ask if you've been taking your meds," Eric says after I take a seat.

"Why?"

"Because you always tell me you are. And I believe you."

"Do you usually believe politicians?"

"No."

I notice that a few Zen posters Eric had hanging on his wall are gone. I'll have to hire a decorator for a guy whose wall is bare. Eric is taking his less-is-more approach a little too far.

"And I won't ask about your fear of failure."

"Why?"

"Because it's gone, or as close to gone as it's going to get. I thought you feared failing the American public. Turns out – with gun control, with you pushing peace in the Middle East, pretty much with everything you do – you only fear doing the wrong thing."

I notice that Eric also has removed the pictures of his wife and son from his desk.

Then, I notice the pictures in a box in the corner along with a Zen placard about change being the only constant in life.

Uh, oh.

"Don't tell me we're breaking up."

"My wife has been on me about moving back to Philadelphia. And, to tell you the truth, I miss the place. My son's graduating college, he'll be out on his own, and it's time I spent more time with my wife."

I'm the President. There should be an executive order I can sign to prevent what is coming up next.

"So, we are breaking up?"

"Let's call it a trial separation. Bottom line, Evan: you don't need to see me so much anymore."

Aside from Tarik, Dr. Carty is the longest-running relationship I have had in my life. Aside from Ariana and my parents, he has done more to mold me into the man I am today than anybody I have ever known.

Are presidents allowed to cry? I don't know, but this president is wiping a tear from his eye.

"Want a Zen saying?" Eric asks. "It's good for what ails you."

"Why not?"

Eric fishes in the box in the corner, pulls out one of his Zen placards and hands it to me.

"*Don't Put a Head on Your Own Head. What's Wrong with Your Own?*" I read. "Most of your Zen stuff, I like, Eric. This, I never could understand."

"It means you should trust yourself. You'll be fine."

And that's that. Thirty-something years of helping me through all of the ups and downs in my life – some more precipitous than others – and Eric will be gone.

We hug.

"Hey," he says. "Keep me on speed dial. I make White House calls."

I feel bad because I won't see him again on a regular basis. I feel good that he trusts me to go on without him.

And I'll feel better if I win the election two days from now.

CHAPTER 85

I feel at home the day before the election because I am at home. My final pitch to the country, my final nationally televised gala and, quite possibly, the final time I'll take the stage as President of the United States will be in Philadelphia.

It's where Mrs. Senesky approached Tarik and I in the schoolyard at Lea Elementary School and told us that she heard there were a couple of "teacher torturers" in our class. Tarik and I thought long and hard about that one but couldn't pin down the culprits. Turned out that Mrs. Senesky was talking about us.

It's where I went to law school. It's where I started dating Ariana. It's where I presided as mayor over a city that molded me before I tried to mold the city.

And it's where we'll have a big, old party tonight on Independence Mall with a national television audience watching, a mall full of supporters cheering and some of my favorite musical artists singing – I still can't believe I got Bonnie Raitt to do this – during the biggest party of my life.

This afternoon, though, I'm sitting in a car munching on cheesesteaks with Tarik, a fleet of Secret Service cars around us, next to a playground in South Philly

"Remember this place?" I ask.

"Remember it? How could I forget?"

Tarik and I used to take mini-road trips around the city, a basketball in the trunk, looking for pickup games. We got our asses handed to us in a game in North Philly one day before deciding to drive to South Philly for dinner and, hopefully, a game against guys we could beat. We won at this playground. And then, just as we're doing today, we wasted all of that healthy exercise by scarfing down a couple of greasy cheesesteaks.

"That jump shot I hit from the corner to win that game here," Tarik says. "It was a thing of beauty.

"You never hit a jump shot from the corner in your life."

Tarik sets his half-eaten cheesesteak down, looks out at the playground and laughs.

"You're right," Tarik says. "You hit the jump shot. I did all the dirty work."

"Just like you do for me now."

Later, in the shadow of Independence Hall and the Liberty Bell and a number of historic buildings I rarely visited before I was elected mayor, the crowd waits for Ariana to deliver her First Lady speech and me to deliver my First Man speech so the Independence Hall revelers can get to the real reason they are here: drinking beer.

First, though, there is Bonnie Raitt. I was a big Beatles fan when I was growing up. Wayne, Tarik, Rick and I would get together in my basement, put on a Beatles record and start air-guitaring along with the music. I always was Paul. Rick, the intellectual of the bunch, was John. Tarik was Ringo, the first and last Black Beatle.

But the Beatles broke up and Bonnie Raitt came into my life when I was a freshman in college. She's been in my life ever since, through at least 20 concerts, through many breakups and through a wedding reception when Ariana and I fought over whether our first dance should be to Bonnie's "Love Me Like a Man."

"Too suggestive," Ariana said then.

"It's what I'll be doing later."

"Not if you play that song."

Bonnie leads with my favorite Bonnie Raitt tune, "Angel from Montgomery." It was written by one of the greatest songwriters of all time, John Prine, who died of COVID in 2020.

I asked her to keep it upbeat and she agreed, playing "Give It Up," and "Something to Talk About." I wanted her to play "Blender Blues," a song about a blender that whips, chops and purees which really isn't about whipping, chopping and pureeing. But Bonnie tells me that it is too sexual and wouldn't go over well in the red states. So, ironically, she plays a heartrending ballad, "I Can't Make You Love Me."

How do you follow that act? You can't, but a number of boring politicians try. And then it's Ariana's turn.

"Hello, Philadelphia! Hello, United States!" Ariana shouts as the crowd cheers. "It feels good to be back in a city where I fell in love with my husband, where I watched him lead this city, where I watched him stiff a bunch of waiters."

Ariana gets more laughs than I usually get.

"Did not!" I yell from the background.

"Actually," Ariana says, "Evan is a good tipper. But they told me to throw a joke into the speech."

Ariana finishes 15 minutes later and it's my turn. I've pretty much said all I can say on the campaign trail, but I try to regurgitate it as painlessly as possible.

"You have a choice tomorrow," I say. "You can choose between one man who voted down a gun bill that would have saved many lives or another man — me, if you're keeping track — who pushed that bill through the House and came pretty darn close in the Senate."

Cheers.

"You can choose between one man, Senator Collins, who looks back on what he calls the good, old days, except they weren't so good for minorities or women or even my Greek immigrant grandparents. Or you can choose another man – me, if you're still keeping track – who looks forward to days that truly will be great for all of us. But we'll only get there if you vote for me. Shameless political plug, I know, but isn't that what this is all about?"

Scattered laughs. Ariana got more.

"I mean this from the bottom of my heart," I conclude. "It has been my honor serving you as President for the last four years. And it will be my great, great honor if you allow me to serve you for four more years. Thank you."

Raucous cheers. A ton of confetti. And a daughter tugging at my sleeve.

"I'd like to say something," Lin says.

"You just being here is enough."

"Not for me, Dad. Can I please say something?"

The politician in me knows it will play well if Lin says what I think she'll say: that I'm a great father, that she loves me, that I always do the right thing.

But the father in me worries. Lin has suffered from social anxiety disorder all of her life and speaking in front of so many people probably isn't recommended for someone who used to have panic attacks before giving book reports.

"Please?"

"All right, honey."

Most of the politicians have left the stage when Lin takes the mike. And most of the people on Independence Mall probably are onto their third beers.

But a hush falls over the crowd when Lin starts.

"I...uh...I...um..."

Shit. The politician in me should have listened to the father in me.

"It's not easy for me speaking in front of so many people," Lin finally says. "But I deal with anxiety issues. I'm a lot better than I used to be. And my Dad, he deals with his bipolar, and he's much, much better than he used to be. In fact, he's much, much better than the other person you could vote for tomorrow. And he's much, much better – I might be a little biased on this – than just about any president we've ever had!"

The silence has turned to cheers.

"I don't know much about politics, so I won't get into that," Lin says. "But I do know that my father is the best man I know. And I know two other things. First, I'll vote for him...."

More cheers.

"And, second, I love him. More than he'll ever know."

Later, Ariana tells me that Lin got the biggest ovation of the night, more than me, more than Ariana, even more than Bonnie.

But I didn't hear it. I was crying my eyes out somewhere on that stage.

CHAPTER 86

I voted for myself. Ariana voted for me. Lin voted for me, although she helped even more with what she said on stage last night.

Two other guys I know would vote for me if they were American citizens, but they are in a safe house in Israel. Still, it was nice hearing from them at 7 a.m. my time and 1 p.m. their time.

"We wish you luck, Mr. President," Noah tells me. "God willing, you still will be in office to help us conclude this peace."

"Is there anything new on your front?"

"Only that Noah and I both share a distaste for chicken kabobs," Farid chimes in. "Why eat chicken when lamb is available?"

Early exit polls show infrastructure as the top issue, mental health second, guns third and the economy fourth. Infrastructure? Who knew? Maybe I should have spent more time talking about building bridges and fixing potholes because that, as it turns out, is what Americans care about. Just because infrastructure bores me doesn't mean it bores the voters.

My Middle East policy came in sixth, according to the exit polls. But fifth – ahead of possible historic peace in the Middle East – was Lin.

"A man whose daughter loves him so much," one voter said when she exited a voting booth in Pennsylvania. "He got my vote."

"Too bad she was born in China," another said. "She'd make a great President."

I'd like to kick back the rest of the day and watch election returns on

PNT, DVTV and VOX. But I can't. Voting hasn't even started out West and has barely started in the Central and Mountain time zones. I still can make a last-minute impression.

"Are you sure you want to spend your entire day in Texas?" Tarik asks, already knowing the answer as we board the plane for Dallas. "They haven't voted for a Democrat since Jimmy Carter in 1976."

"That was way before Parkview. And those 40 electoral votes would come in handy."

We touch down at Dallas Fort Worth International Airport and my caravan makes a beeline for AT&T Stadium, where the Dallas Cowboys play. The last time I was in Texas to watch a Cowboys game was 1976 when I watched them pummel the Eagles. Good thing they didn't have cell phones in those days, or somebody would have recorded a video of me getting beer dumped on my head after I might have said a few nasty things to Cowboys fans.

I'll try to be nice today. I'll *really, really* try even though the Cowboys still are a thorn in the Eagles side.

"How 'bout them Cowboys!" I shout to a fairly large throng of people at the stadium. If polls didn't show that I had a fairly big lead in Pennsylvania, I probably would have used a different line to start my speech. "But, seriously, y'all know that I'm an Eagles fan. Still, how can you hate greatness? The 'Boys have won five Super Bowls. The Eagles have won one."

I probably should stick with Cowboys talk. Hell, all Democratic candidates that follow me should stick with Cowboys talk. I get huge cheers and don't have to see exit polls to know that the Cowboys, more so than infrastructure, rank highest on Texans' minds.

Where's Tarik? He's usually up here on stage with me, but I saw him talking with a guy in a fancy suit and cowboy hat when we entered the stadium and haven't seen him since.

No big deal. I still have Ariana to guide me.

"'Y'all'?" she whispers in my ear as I wait for the cheers to die down. "I never heard you use the word."

"I never had to win Texas as much as I do today."

I see plenty of anti-gun signs in the crowd. "*Stop the Violence.*" "*Safe Gun Laws.*" "*Too Many Dead.*" But I see just as many signs indicating that Texas voters might not be willing for a sea change. "*Keep Your Hands off My Second Amendment.*" "*Too Bad Teachers Don't Carry Guns.*" And an old standard: "*Guns Don't Kill People; People Kill People.*"

I'll have to win over the Second Amendment people if I have any chance to win this state – and, from what polls tell me leading up to the election – the presidency. So, I address my comments to them.

"I love the Second Amendment," I say. "I just don't like the way it has been twisted by politicians to include assault rifles, hollow point bullets, the things that left all of those kids dead in Parkview and leave all of our fine policemen dead when they pull people over for running red lights."

Sounds reasonable to me. But it might not sound good on the news to anti-gun voters if the video stops after my first sentence.

"Y'all want the same thing I do. Y'all want safer streets, safer schools, safer homes. I don't want to take away that gun you have at home to protect yourselves from the burglar who breaks in. But I sure as hell want to take the guns out of the hands of people who walk into schools and kill innocent children and use policemen for target practice."

More cheers, though not as loud as the ones I got with my Dallas Cowboys remarks. But I'll take it. If we can pick off a number of Texas voters, we just might have a shot at this state. And if we take Texas, we'll win the whole thing.

"Three 'y'alls?" Ariana says as I walk off the stage. "Want me to fix you up a plate of grits?"

Finally, I see Tarik. He's talking to the same man he was talking to when we entered the stadium. He ends that conversation in time to hop in the back seat of a car that will take us to the airport.

"Who was that?" I ask.

"Somebody who could put you over the top in this state."

"How?"

Tarik smiles.

"How 'bout them Cowboys!" he says. "You know, we usually buy Eagles season tickets. Lose this thing and we might be last on the waiting list."

CHAPTER 87

As I'm switching from PNT to DVTV to VOX on election night, not so much to see the results but because I'm nervous and have to give my hands something to do, I keep thinking of Harry Truman.

"He went to sleep on election night," I tell Ariana. "Told the Secret Service to wake him up if anything important happened."

"They didn't have cable in those days."

"Man must have had the greatest therapist in the world. Or the greatest sleeping pills in the world. Or both."

I have a great therapist in Eric Carty. I don't take sleeping pills. I can only hope that the election today turns out as well for me as it did for Truman in 1948 when he upset Thomas Dewey.

It looks good in the beginning, but I expected it to look good in the beginning. The polls closed in the Eastern states first and, as expected, I took New York and its 29 electoral votes while building an early lead over Collins.

"And you know President Pappas will take California and its 55 electoral votes later," Bekka Mornay tells the five other DVTV panelists at the election coverage desk. "Will President Pappas, who pulled off a minor miracle four years ago by winning as an Independent, win again?"

"As Biggie said, 'Growing up in the streets of Bed-Stuy, it was hard, yo,'" Melman says.

"Huh?"

I have to hand it to Melman. Election night, arguably the biggest night in America every four years, and he stays on brand. But I'm guessing he could have stayed on brand with a more apt rap lyric.

I take one Southern state, Georgia, which experienced three mass shootings over the last year.

"A Democrat winning Georgia, not completely unexpected," Tanner says. "President Pappas has been pushing for safe gun legislation and the Peach State knows the pain of the gun legislation we have in place now."

The rest of the South isn't so kind. Alabama, Mississippi and Louisiana help Collins surge into a temporary lead before I pick off a couple of swing states to leave us in a virtual dead heat midway through the night.

"Maybe you should have trotted out a couple more 'y'alls' when you were on your Southern whistle stop tour," Ariana says. "You would have won by now."

The talking heads go back and forth about the impact of me announcing that I was bipolar.

"He should have kept it to himself until after the election," Brolin Murphy says on VOX.

"One word to describe what he did politically: crazy," Brett Bishop says. And the VOX talking heads, even the token liberal, laugh.

I make a mental note not to send VOX news personalities Christmas cards.

My Middle East initiative is playing well in the Northern states, according to exit polls, and is a negative in Southern states. My gun stance is a positive overall, according to those same exit polls, with all of these school shootings so fresh in the public's mind. And then there's Lin.

"What bravery that young woman displayed on the night before the election," Tanner says. "If her father wins, he should raise her allowance."

"Did you get an allowance when you were 20, Jack?" one of his colleagues asks.

"How do you think I paid for law school?"

Ariana wants to cuddle. I oblige but am not fully invested. Brolin and Ari have my attention.

"Later. If I win," I tell her.

"And if you lose?"

"Same deal."

James Asher sends up a tray of lobster rolls and I gobble down three quickly. I'm not sure I'll squeeze into my suit later – whether I'm delivering a concession or acceptance speech – but Asher's lobster rolls are worth it.

"All eyes are on Texas," Mornay says after one of her colleagues does his frenetic electoral map thing. "President Pappas takes it, he wins. He loses, like so many Democratic candidates before him, and Senator Collins will be President of the United States."

"It's like Tupac said...."

"Shut up, Ari."

I actually fall asleep. Four lobster rolls, chased down by a couple of brandies, will do that to you. Maybe that was Truman's secret.

Ariana doesn't wake me. She's good like that. She didn't even wake me on our sixth date when she invited me up to her apartment for the first time. I fell fast asleep fully clothed on her couch after a night at Frankie's Irish Bar in West Philly.

"Honey." Is that Ariana or am I dreaming?

"Oh, honey." That's definitely Ariana but I don't want to open my eyes and hear that I lost.

But the suspense and my stomach – I ate too much – are killing me.

"Honey."

"Yes."

"You won."

I look at the clock. It's 3 a.m. and PNT just called the election for me.

"You won, honey."

I hug Ariana after I wipe the sleep from my eyes. I dance around the room with her, James Brown funking out on "Super Bad" in the background. I want to pull Ariana under the presidential covers but can't because there's somebody on Line 1.

"Congratulations, Mr. President." It's Trey Collins. We've gone hard after each other during the campaign but he sounds genuinely gracious. "We disagree on most things, but we both love this country. Do right by her, Mr. President. Do right by her."

"Thank you, Trey."

I'm ready to hang up until I realize Collins isn't finished.

"That ad you ran today in Texas, it won it for you," he says.

"What ad?"

"Come on, Mr. President. You know. The one that showed dead bodies. The one that showed me holding a smoking gun. And you're supposed to be the moral one? But, hey, I guess that's politics."

It's not the type of politics I wanted to practice in order to ensure four more years in the White House, though.

But I'll worry about that later. For now, I have to squeeze into a suit and deliver a victory speech to a cheering crowd at the Algonquin Hotel.

"Want another lobster roll?" Ariana says as she comes out of the bedroom wearing a stunning First Lady dress.

"I can barely fit into this suit as it is."

"You're President. The voters already voted. It doesn't matter if your suit's too tight."

She's right. For now, I want to enjoy the moment. I'm President of the United States, damn it. I'm President of the United States.

"I'll take that lobster roll, honey. What the hell."

CHAPTER 88

Ariana and I start the day after the election the way we started the day before the election: watching cable TV.

Turns out that America wasn't ready to accept a president with bipolar, but not enough to keep me out of the White House for a second term. Exit polls showed that 53 percent of voters considered my bipolar a negative, 43 percent said it didn't matter and the rest, probably psychiatrists whose client list will double, said it was a plus.

"It's progress," Josh Madras says on PNT. "But we still have a long way to go."

Ariana nudges me.

"Can you fetch me a cup of coffee," she asks.

"You expect the president – two terms, mind you – to fetch coffee?"

Ariana doesn't say a word. She doesn't have to. I go to the kitchen, get her a cup of coffee – no sugar, heavy cream – and come back to bed.

"I switched to DVTV," Ariana says. "Can't wait to see what Melman has to say about your win."

But Melman doesn't mention Tupac. Or Biggie. Or any of the other rap artists or lyrics I don't know. Ari Melman has switched to an old crooner. But he isn't reciting the lyrics. My decision to announce I am bipolar has spurred Ari to sing them.

"*And more, much, much more,*" Ari sings, not even coming close to Sinatra, "*I did it my way.*"

"Can we get back to Tupac?" Mornay asks.

"I thought you didn't like a middle-aged White guy trying to be cool."

"I don't. But that's the worst Sinatra I ever heard."

Pretty much every cable station came back with the same exit poll numbers. My stance on guns was a positive. It wouldn't have been a positive four years ago, but we hadn't lived through Parkview and way too many other mass murders.

The Middle East? A slight negative, voters wanting me to focus more on problems in this country than problems abroad. I want to scream at the TV -- *"But we're on the verge of a lasting peace!"* -- but decide to save my voice for the many speeches I'll deliver later.

"The Lin Factor," which is what all of the networks are calling it, probably gave me the small bump I needed in my 10-electoral vote win.

"Article II, Section 1," Ariana says. "You oughta' do something about it."

"Why?"

"Lin would make a good president, and Article II, Section I won't let her do it because she was born in China."

"What makes you think she'd want to be President?"

"True. Too much lying."

Gladys is at the office even though I told her to take the day off. But there she is behind her desk, stacks of envelopes in front of her, telling callers that "I'll tell him when he comes in" with me standing right in front of her.

"Here," she says. "Take these."

I take the handful of envelopes, shut the door to the Oval Office and start to read at my desk, yet another cup of coffee in front of me to make up for a long, presidential partying night.

From Aida Sterling, Parkview, Texas: "I'll never get my daughter back. Just make sure other mothers aren't sitting here, alone, like me."

I'll try, Aida. I'll try. But with people like Collins sitting in the Senate, it will be difficult.

And this from Dr. Eric Carty, Philadelphia, Pennsylvania: "What's next? Emperor? Master of the Universe? Congratulations. And keep taking your meds."

Some of my sports heroes – Allen Iverson, Andrew Toney and Doug Peterman – sent congratulations. Some of my musical heroes – Bonnie Raitt, Taj Mahal, Joni Mitchell – sent congratulations. I'd prefer concert tickets. And there are some from world leaders, even Russian dictator Vladimir Putin, who writes that he looks forward to me agreeing with him every step along the way.

Conspicuous by their congratulatory absence are Noah and Farid. I figure they have worked long into the night putting the final touches on a peace agreement and will call when they're finished.

I learn early in the afternoon that I am dead wrong.

CHAPTER 89

Noah tells me later that he sleeps like a baby. It is a skill honed years ago when he was a member of the Israeli Defense Forces fighting on the front lines with bombs bursting around him.

"If you don't sleep," he tells me as I talk to him by phone from the Oval Office, "you can't focus. If you can't focus, you die."

But that's not why Noah couldn't sleep last night. And it isn't because he was watching American television wondering whether I won the election or whether he would have to deal with Collins in January.

It was because he finally came up with a way to nail down a peace plan he has been working on with Farid for months.

"I do not know if it came to me in a dream, whether it was my subconscious working overtime or whether it was a too-sweet piece of baklava Farid and I shared earlier," Noah says. "But I awoke, raced downstairs and started typing away on my computer."

The sticking point in what Noah and Farid wanted to be a lasting peace was education. Both agreed that Palestinian schools had to stop teaching hate. Both agreed that it all starts with the children, and peace couldn't be maintained if Palestinian children were taught to hate Israelis early and taught to kill Israelis later.

But they disagreed on implementation. Farid wanted Palestinians to take charge with Israeli educators – not ineffectual U.N. overseers – dropping in monthly. Noah wanted Israelis running the classrooms.

"But I was missing something" Noah tells me. "The solution all along was two teachers in each classroom. One Israeli, one Palestinian, each with shared responsibilities. It seems simple, but it took a bad piece of baklava for me to see it."

And to input his thoughts on a computer after he excitedly ran down the stairs at the safe house.

"Peace," Noah says. "Peace. It's all I ever wanted. And Farid, it's all he wanted, too."

That's when Noah heard the first shot. And then the second.

And that is when he heard his wife scream.

He raced upstairs to find Sarah, alive. He embraced her but his happiness didn't last long.

Sarah pointed toward the room Farid shared with his close friend and advisor, Khalafi Shardoom. Noah knew what he would find before he opened the door but opened it anyway.

There, sitting up in bed with a gun at his side, was Shardoom. Blood was splattered on the wall behind him and was soaking into the pillows. Shardoom was dead of an apparent suicide.

And there, slumped at a desk in the corner, was Farid. Blood was pooling on the floor. Blood was pooling on a document in front of Farid, who apparently was doing a little late-night work on the peace proposal when Shardoom shot him before taking his own life.

"Call the doctor," Noah yelled, searching for a pulse when he checked Farid. "Call the doctor. Now!"

But it was too late. Farid and Shardoom were dead when the doctor arrived and prospects for peace in the Middle East might have died with them.

Noah tells me that Shardoom always seemed uncomfortable with talk of peace. But he was Farid's childhood friend. "My most trusted friend,"

Farid had said. And Noah went along with it.

Israeli intelligence learned in the hours after Farid's death, Noah tells me, that one of Shardoom's sisters died in Israel's counterattack after Jakub. Israeli intelligence also found that Shardoom had contact with an Islamic Jihad leader two weeks earlier.

"They got to him," Noah says. And I think I hear a tough, grizzled war veteran crying on the other end. "They got to Shardoom. And Shardoom got to my friend."

Twenty-four hours ago, I won the election.

As I sit here now, I don't feel like I won. I don't feel like the world won.

"Is there a way to continue the peace talks?" I ask.

"We can continue to talk," Noah says. "But Farid was the only Palestinian willing to listen. The only leader in this whole region willing to listen."

They were so close. So close. Now, Israel and Palestine are back where they started.

"I am being rude," Noah says before he ends the call. "Congratulations on your win."

Yeah. Congratulations.

EPILOGUE

Come on, man, let's hoop," Tarik says. "It'll get you out of this funk. Especially if I let you beat me."

It has been two days since I learned of Farid's death, and I haven't left the White House except to do a couple of obligatory I-won-the-election speeches and photo ops.

I'm President again, but what makes me think I can change anything when I couldn't change anything in the Middle East the first time around?

"A quick game to 11," Tarik says. "I'll spot you five points."

Fifteen minutes later, we're standing at the top of the key on the White House court. I'm holding the ball, unable to get Farid's death out of my mind.

"Did I miss something?" I ask.

"Miss this shot and I'll run the table."

"Big, bad American president. Here I am, thinking I can broker a peace, and the Palestinians and Israelis, the people who know more about this thing than I'll ever know, are still at war."

"Just shoot the damn shot. And, no, you didn't miss anything."

We start.

Tarik is focused more on the game than I am, which is one of the reasons he scores 10 straight point. He only needs one more basket to notch his latest win in a rivalry that has lasted almost as long as the Sixers-Celtics.

"Just don't elbow me on the way to the hoop," I tell Tarik, handing him the ball.

"When did I ever use my elbows?" Tarik asks, maintaining a straight face.

"In Texas."

We talked Texas and Tarik's meeting with the man in the suit the day after the election. Tarik told me that he was a Parkview parent who wanted to get Tarik's approval before he ran an attack ad. I told Tarik that he should have come to me. Tarik told me that he doesn't come to me with a lot of things. "Plausible deniability," Tarik calls it. I call it not wanting to hear "no" for an answer.

I've seen the ad, and it was every bit as bad as Collins made it sound when he called to concede the election. The actor playing Collins was holding a smoking gun. He had blood pooled at his feet. The ad didn't use numbers to detail how many died at Parkview. It showed Collins stacking bodies.

"You would have said no if I told you about it," Tarik explained.

"You're damn right."

"And you probably wouldn't be President today."

Tarik probably is right about that, too. Which would mean that the body count during Collins' first term would rise, Americans would retreat into a Middle Ages view on mental health and the country would be screwed for four, maybe eight, years.

You have to break some eggs to make an omelet. Tarik broke some eggs. I like omelets.

"Want me to beat you with a jump shot from the corner?" Tarik asks.

"I've said it before and I'll say it again: you've never made a corner jumper in your life."

He does this time, though. He's Chief of Staff for another four years. I guess the election boosted his confidence.

"You won. Happy?" I ask.

"We won. And, yes, I'm happy."

I get four years to work on safer gun laws, safer streets and the economy. I also have four more years to work on peace in the Middle East, although my recent experience tells me it will take a lot longer than that.

But I'll worry about those issues later. For now, I am the 22nd two-term president in U.S history.

Let me amend that. I am the first President who declared he was bipolar before going out and winning an election. Things could be better. But things could be a hell of a lot worse.

ABOUT THE AUTHOR

Chris Morkides, a mental health counselor since 2008, has been enriched as much by his clients as he hopes he has enriched their lives. Nobody is braver, Mr. Morkides feels, than people who stare down their mental health issues every day.

Mr. Morkides decided in 2019, though, that he wanted to devote most of his professional life to writing. He already had written about Kobe Bryant, Philadelphia pro, college and high school teams and the occasional zoning hearing board meeting – when he could stay awake – for the *Philadelphia Inquirer* and various magazines and wanted to tackle writing a novel.

Despite reservations – *I don't have that many words in me!* – Mr. Morkides started on his first novel, *Trust Me*. He finished it by paying attention to the words of one of his few non-family heroes, Thich Nhat Hahn. The late Nobel Prize nominee and anti-war activist told us to eat a tangerine one section at a time. Eating one section at a time – writing a little every day – Mr. Morkides combined therapy, suspense and psychology to finish *Trust Me*. Mr. Morkides had become a big tangerine fan by the time he finished his first book and went on to write *Good Intentions*, the second novel in the Alex Johns Series. He recently finished the third installment in the series, *Fouled*.

Mr. Morkides loves traveling – to Paris, especially – his Philadelphia sports teams, playing Scrabble on-line, shooting hoops when his creaky knees allow and, especially, spending time with his wife, Alisa, and daughter, Kina.

He also enjoys reading, although Kina is the biggest reader in the family. James Lee Burke, Elmore Leonard and Dennis Lehane are his favorites in the crime/suspense genre. Frederick Backman makes him stray from that genre often, though.

To contact Mr. Morkides, feel free to email at cmorkides@aol.com.

282